Vitality Means Church Growth

Creative Leadership Series

Vitality Means Church Growth

Douglas W. Johnson

Creative Leadership Series
Lyle E. Schaller, Editor

Abingdon Press/Nashville

VITALITY MEANS CHURCH GROWTH

Copyright © 1989 by Abingdon Press

This book is printed on acid-free paper.

Library of Congress Cataloging-in-Publication Data

JOHNSON, DOUGLAS W., 1934—
    Vitality means church growth.
    (Creative leadership series)
    1. Church renewal. 2. Church growth.
I. Title. II. Series.
BV600.2.J574 1989   253   88-34399

ISBN 0-687-43799-7 (alk. paper)

MANUFACTURED BY THE PARTHENON PRESS AT
NASHVILLE, TENNESSEE, UNITED STATES OF AMERICA

Foreword

Back in 1890, fewer than one-half of the 160,000 Christian congregations in the United States had been in existence for as long as twenty-five years, and approximately one-fifth had been in existence for less than a decade.

A hundred years later the ecclesiastical landscape is dominated by long established congregations. At least 80 percent of the estimated 400,000 congregations in the United States and Canada were established before 1965. In several of the oldline Protestant denominations well over 95 percent of today's churches were founded before 1965.

One result of this aging of the congregations on this continent can be seen in the large number of churches that report a shrinking number of members. New congregations are far more likely to experience numerical growth than long established parishes.

A second consequence is revealed by denominational statistics. Those religious bodies, including several that vehemently reject being identified as a denomination, which report that at least one-third of their congregations were established during the past two decades also usually report an increase in the total membership. Those denominational families which report that fewer than one-tenth of their congregations are less than twenty-five years old usually report a decline in the total number of members. That appears to be more than simply a coincidence!

A third product of this maturing of so many congregations is institutional blight. Like all other institutions in our society, churches are vulnerable to the blight of becoming self-centered, of turning means-to-an-end concerns—such as real estate and finances—into ends in themselves, and of repelling the people the institution originally was created to serve. In some cases the decision was made to add paid staff to help implement mission, but today one of the reasons for retaining certain staff positions is to provide employment for one or two or three adults who would have difficulty finding another job.

Long established institutions tend to lose their vitality and to focus on survival goals. This is a normal, natural, and predictable pattern that can be seen in the United States Congress, in philanthropic agencies, in educational institutions, and in military organizations as well as in profit making businesses.

That is the subject of this book. Douglas W. Johnson contends that by the nature of their being Christian, congregations should display a vitality that both nurtures the members and attracts newcomers. Vitality has replaced denominational loyalties and kinship ties today as the critical factor in attracting new members. As the author points out, mature congregations often tend to make it easy for members to become complacent and drift aimlessly.

This book both defines the nature of vital congregations and describes the distinctive characteristics of vital churches. One of these is broad lay involvement in ministry. That is *not* the same as strong lay involvement in administration, as is pointed out repeatedly in this book. Another is the energetic, creative, and enthusiastic pastor who is comfortable working with strong lay leadership. A third is the quality and variety of the program.

This volume stands out from other books concerned with congregational renewal for three distinct reasons.

The first, and by far the most impressive, contribution of the book is the broad data base for the author's diagnosis and prescriptions. This is not simply the autobiographical account of one minister or of one congregation. This book is based on a broad collection of data drawn from many congregations of various sizes, types, and labels.

The second distinctive contribution is that Dr. Johnson speaks to leaders from churches of all sizes and types. This is a product of that broad data base, but it also has enabled the author to identify factors that are close to universal. Regardless of the size of your congregation, this book speaks to concerns on your agenda as you struggle with the question of vitality.

Third, as any reader will discover very quickly, this book is grounded in reality. Too often books on congregational renewal cause the reader to conclude, "There is zero overlap between the world I live in and this book!" This volume is based on the real world and speaks to real people in the real world who are seeking help in revitalizing their church.

Like other books in the Creative Leadership Series, this volume is directed to both the laity and the clergy and can be used productively with a discovery-type self-study group or long range planning committee.

Lyle E. Schaller
Yokefellow Institute
Richmond, Indiana

Contents

Preface

This book is for pastors and local church leaders who want a vital church. It is based on research studies that sought from pastors and lay persons the basic characteristics of a vital congregation. The first of these studies, *Congregations As Units of Mission*, was a nationwide study, while the second, *A Study of Vital Churches*, was a more detailed look at 160 congregations. The third study consisted of interviews with pastors and eight laypersons in a total of thirty-two United Methodist and United Church of Christ congregations.

Many people helped make it possible to complete these studies, including Community Workers of the National program Division of the General Board of Global Ministries of The United Methodist Church, Robert Burt of the United Church of Christ, Rene O. Bideaux, Deputy General Secretary of the National Program Division, and Lyle E. Schaller. To each of these persons I owe many thanks. Very helpful and gracious were the pastors and laypersons who responded in the various studies on which this book is based.

Vitality is so much nicer than uncertainity and despair. Chronicling the attributes of these vital churches is an attempt to encourage congregations to take the steps necessary to become vital. May God be in your hearts.

Douglas W. Johnson
April 1988

Introduction

The music is flowing and people in the rear of the sanctuary are greeting one another as they look for their favorite pews.

"Hello. I'm Joe Fields. Glad to see you. You're new, aren't you?"

"Hi! I'm Cathy Leones. Yes. I'm new in town and was looking for a church. This one was easy to find."

"I'm glad of that, and I'm happy to have you come to worship with us. I hope you like what happens here this morning. May I show you to a seat?"

This usher demonstrates one of the prerequisites people search for in a church: a feeling of being welcome and of being recognized as important. When most people walk into a church, they are hoping to find a congregation that gives them a feeling of welcome. They also are looking for a sense of religious aliveness and vitality within the people in the church. Ask a visitor to describe what is meant by religious or spiritual aliveness and vitality and he or she will talk about "friendliness," "warmth," "good music," "good preaching," and "concern for me as a person."

These are very subjective descriptions. They have to do

15

with past experiences of church life as well as current personal needs. Yet, these are the bases on which individuals judge whether or not to attend a particular church. They are seeking a place that can assist them in finding purpose and meaning in life as well as help them discover new ways to cope with life's difficulties and problems. These needs in their own lives are played out in the demands they place upon a church. They want it to be important to them.

People are not guided by denominational loyalties so much now as they may have been in the past. They have trouble explaining their spiritual needs, but these needs are quite real. They are looking for vital churches, which, according to their definitions, are congregations that can assist in their search for deeper religious meanings in their own lives, can guide them in using their time and skills to help others, and can provide them with a network of other people who can support and care for them during some of life's sharpest moments.

It would be great if all churches did those things for every person who came through their doors! Unfortunately, only a small percentage of the churches fulfill criteria for being vital. Yet, congregations really wanting to be vital and challenging can be just that. There is no magic or any special requirements for becoming vital. Vitality is within the reach of any church. Most of the requirements for being vital can be met by developing and nurturing a strong and active layperson network and encouraging and supporting a pastor who helps create invigorating worship, broad ranging programs, and is a leader in mission to the community and to the world.

The Search for Vital Churches

Much recent interest has been expressed in describing vital churches. This is not a new search, although it seems to be more pressing now than in former times. One possible reason for the current search may be due to the maturity or age of many congregations. In most congregations that have been established for many years, present members have not had to formulate the purposes for mission and ministry or work to create a spiritual fellowship. The members came into a church that had its purpose, programs, mission, and fellowship activities already in place. The longer a church has been established, the more often it tends to forget that its members need the opportunity and challenge of creating anew the basis for its life, mission, and ministry. In these studies, vitality began when members began to struggle with setting up the purposes, programs, mission, and fellowship for their church's ministry and mission.

Interest in how churches become vital has become acute because some church leaders believe that once discovered, indicators of vitality can be transferred to other less vibrant churches. The result would be a whole passel of vital churches that could result in growing denominations.

One of the fears of many church leaders about the emphasis on church growth is that its primary goal is on numbers and not on the spiritual growth and development of converts and members. The quality of a congregation, for these leaders, is more important than the quantity of people involved in programs. Yet, church leaders often are not interested in making this distinction between quality and quantity because in the recent past, many pastors used a personal interpretation of "quality" as an excuse for not working. Such pastors felt that taking controversial stands was enough of a witness. Consequently, they did not provide the leadership necessary for their churches to emphasize the essentials of strong worship and pastoral care. One consequence of this limited definition of "quality" has been a serious decline in membership in those churches.

A combination of quantity and quality in a church's program and attitude is critical before that church can become a vital congregation. Vital churches have a message about Jesus Christ's love and life that members can't contain within themselves. Members of vital churches have an excitement about their lives and their faith commitments that grip others. They become activists in the faith. These attributes are attractive to many persons who have been without the church for a long time. They see the vitality of the church members and want to share in whatever it is that turns those people on.

A church with vitality can become diseased and die. Being vital is like living; death is always present. Vitality must be practiced and cultivated if it is to survive. A spiritual dynamic must be developed and maintained. This means that churches must not be protective so much as they must be practitioners of vitality. Churches must build on and use vitality in order to keep and strengthen it. Vitality must be nurtured and tested in order to grow.

The Intent of the Book

The intent of this book is to share insights from congregations that have indices of vitality. These churches were selected on the basis of studies and are a sample of many other congregations whose programs and activities bring hope, love, and meaning to members and nonmembers in their communities. The experiences of this sample are a microcosm of the varied and exciting lives of many churches across the world.

The characteristics of a vital congregation are as follows. (1) A vital church has a strong lay leadership group that feels responsible for the church and its program. These lay leaders represent a wide spectrum of the membership and hold office for relatively short periods of time. (2) The vital church is distinguished by its programs of Christian education, including adult Christian education, stewardship, and a mission program that stretches the interests of its members beyond the confines of the building. (3) Vital congregations have worship experiences that excite attendees and speak to the needs and possibilities of being a Christian. These services include a variety of types of music. (4) Vital congregations have pastors who are energetic, creative, and are able to allow and encourage lay participation in the full range of programs and activities. These attributes are the basis for the book's descriptions.

The book is descriptive. It seeks to put before lay leaders and pastors the kinds of activities and programs vital churches engage in and support. It describes what makes churches exciting and useful. The descriptions are based on actual churches, their programs, and their people.

Possible Uses of the Book

Chapter 8, the last chapter of the book, is a collection of leading questions. You may use them to examine your own church, or they may be used in small group study as stimulants for discussion. It is anticipated that the experiences of other churches may encourage and guide readers to find and to strengthen additional elements of vitality in their own congregations.

The questions are discussion starters and are not intended to be the only questions a church must answer if it is to become vital. Planning processes have been used by several of the churches studied as a stepping off place for a new sense of vitality. Guides for church planning processes are available from regional and national denominational offices.

In addition to these questions, the discussion in each

chapter is presented in a practical manner. This is done so that church leaders and members have handles for immediate action.

Illustrations in the book are experiences of specific congregations. While it is difficult to take the experience of another church and assume that events will occur in the same way in yours, those experiences may be stimulants for your creating new opportunities for mission and ministry in your congregation. The experience of one church can be quite instructive to others because most congregations have similar purposes and attempt to fulfill somewhat the same needs.

The Structure of the Book

The book begins with a discussion of the importance of lay involvement and concludes with a discussion of the role of the pastor. The other chapters are arranged according to their importance in creating and sustaining a vital church. None of the themes can be separated from the others. Vitality is a mix of these themes in the context of the persons and situation of the church.

In most of the congregations studied, an event precipitated vitality, but this was perceived after the fact, not at the time of the event. Empowering and exciting laypersons through study and presentation of the gospel was the trigger for vitality in most of the congregations studied. They came alive because of their involvement in some major new thrust in the life of the church.

Pastors of vital congregations have assumed very delimited, but crucial, roles. They are not all things to everyone. They are worship leaders, trainers, innovators, challengers, and pastors. They are persons who offer new opportunities for ministry and mission to church leaders. In this respect, they are stimulators for innovation and change. The limitations placed on the pastor's role require a special type of person to serve in a vital church. However, many clergy can adapt their style to these role needs.

It is with lay involvement in the life of vital churches that we begin the discussion.

I

Vital Congregations

Steeples break up the skylines of cities and countrysides across the nation. In the churches under these steeples, people are living experiences of faith and hope in situations not always uplifting and positive. Clergy are seeking to lead even when they feel frustrated and inept in their leadership roles. This is the church. It is a human institution blessed with a message of divine inspiration and hope. Much of the time, the humanness of the institution obscures its mission. Many churches are in ministries that focus on their survival and are mired in their own pettiness. So many churches are in this category that some people feel the church has lost the vitality of its unique mission and ministry. That's not true. Many other congregations have responded with commitment and service to the call of God. These churches are alive and vital. They can be models to other congregations seeking to follow the Christ in a world not yet ready for his message.

Vital congregations have an aura and a message that other congregations would like to have. A major problem in trying to transfer vitality from one congregation to another is understanding how vitality is achieved. Descriptions of six congregations provide basic models that will inform our discussion of the primary characteristics of vitality in the church. These models become the reference point for churches seeking to become vital or more vital in their own ministry and mission.

First Church: Small City

Small City has had a population of about 75,000 people for the past two decades. The city is surrounded by farmland, although some of this has been sold for commercial and industrial development during the past five years. Because of its location the area has been beset with economic problems associated with farming, but it is seeking to diversify its economy by attracting industry and is looking forward to fewer of the ups and downs associated with a single economic base. The first shopping mall was built about a decade ago, and four new malls have been added during the past five years. Office space has been constructed near the malls for two new medical groups.

First Church is located two blocks from the main downtown intersection in the center of this city. Although the church's members have discussed the possibility of moving it out along one of the highways into an area of potential growth, they decided to remain in their present location. The church has had a historic position of ministry in the community, and the members felt that a move would not be useful. They believe the church is needed and can serve best where it is currently situated.

First Church's current membership is about 750, with an average attendance of 380 at its two services on Sunday morning. Parking is a bit tight, but one of the new city parking lots is nearby and is available for use on Sunday morning. This has relieved a potentially troublesome issue.

24

The Sunday school has varied in size during the past few years, but currently 310 are enrolled and 157 attend on an average Sunday. During the past year, efforts have been made to increase adult education offerings with a result that two new adult classes have been formed. Also, elementary age attendance, especially in the preschool and kindergarten classes, has increased. A possible reason for this increase is that the new adult classes have attracted young parents.

The church's budget in 1988 was supported by an average of $400 per member. It has fluctuated somewhat because of the economic conditions of the community, but the budget is affected more by the church's emphasis on giving than by economic changes in the community. In years when the church has a strong stewardship campaign, focusing on finances, giving increases. This past year the church had a strong emphasis on financial stewardship.

A new pastor came two years ago. This was the first time the church had had a pastor who was in his early forties. He came at an opportune time. The former pastor, although beloved, had served beyond his effectiveness. The church had been in "neutral" during the last three years of his tenure. The new pastor came into a setting of hope and expectation and has helped the church become more focused in its ministry and mission. Partly because of his age (the age of the minister often is reflected in the age of newcomers into the congregation), he has been able to attract younger couples and singles into active participation in the congregation.

The church has had a history of strong lay leadership. Unlike some congregations that have problems because lay leaders are resistant to any type of change, the lay leaders in this church have worked hard to develop a sense of mission and ministry for the congregation. They have attended conferences and training sessions to learn and to be inspired. They have read and studied booklets, provided by the denomination, aimed at assisting them to be better leaders. They have worked with the pastor to create a statement of purpose and mission for the congregation.

The program of the church is varied. Outreach into the community has included support for the local food bank and regular contributions to various help groups in the city. Some members have been involved in work camps in other parts of the United States, and three persons went last year to a work camp in Bolivia. Those volunteering to help in work camps have been financially supported by the congregation.

A mission fair is held each year. This consists of bringing to the church one or two of the overseas missionaries it supports. Other missionaries serve within the United States in urban missions as well as in a rural mission in a neighboring county. Money for missions is raised partly through a faith promise campaign.

Sunday morning worship has an exciting quality about it. The adult choir has increased in size from ten to thirty people, primarily because of the new choir director. Music is quite varied, with soloists ranging from very good to somewhat good. The important ingredient in the worship experience is the vibrancy of the leaders and the enthusiasm of the choirs (there are four of them). The pastor's sermons are rated as very good and helpful.

One aspect of the church's program that seems to have been particularly helpful has been the decision to require a tenure system for leaders. This system was put in place despite considerable strain and discomfort among some long-term leaders. However, they have become accustomed to it, and most now are strong supporters of the concept. One reason for their support has been the requirement that those who have taken time off from leading become involved in another aspect of the church's program as a participant. A few of these "on leave" leaders have joined a Bethel Bible Series study course of two years. A planning committee has been in place for the past two years and is helping the church look seriously at the needs it can address in its mission and ministry. The people in the church are excited about it and what they are doing through the church.

Trinity Church: Suburbia

Various types of suburban areas exist, but this community is in a growing area. It is on the edge of a midsouth metropolitan area that is attracting developers who are creating subdivisions and shopping centers. The population has mushroomed by 10,000 during the last five years. The new residents include older persons who have moved into an apartment complex for retired people just across the street from the church. Single family homes for more affluent buyers have sprung up in the developments that have been interspersed among neighborhoods of older single family homes. Shopping malls and office buildings are along the highway in front of the church. The highway, because of these developments, has become a strip of barriers tending to isolate various neighborhoods from one another.

Trinity Church was started in the early 1970s and, after a relatively slow start, has grown rapidly. The current membership is 1,975 with an average attendance of 560. The size of the sanctuary has limited the ability of the church to increase the attendance at worship. Both services have been filled to capacity. This limitation of sanctuary space led to a decision by the pastor and the board to have three services each Sunday morning plus their Sunday evening service. The introduction of the new service schedule has been recent, so its effect on the average attendance has not been felt fully.

The Sunday school enrolled 1,000 this past year with an average of 480 in attendance. Adult education is an important part of the Sunday school. Three new classes, plus a singles ministry, were begun during the past year. The church staff has grown along with the membership. A senior pastor, two full-time associates, a director of Christian education, a director of music, an organist, and a part-time pastor of visitation comprise the professional staff. Two secretaries, a part-time business manager, and a coordinator of volunteers are laypersons on the staff. Two janitors complete the staff for the church. A part-time youth director, a student at a nearby seminary, is hired during the school year. In addition, a corps of volunteers is used in the office on a regular basis.

The community in which the church is located is rather affluent, which is reflected in the amount of money contributed to the church. The expenditures in 1988 were about $625 per member, which included support for six full-time professional staff plus the support staff members. Discussions about purchasing adjacent land for construction of new buildings and parking space are now in process. The primary needs are for more parking, classrooms, and a larger sanctuary.

This congregation, similar to others, has a Wednesday night church supper followed by programs and meetings. This supper is prepared and served by one of the groups in the church under the direction of a hostess-coordinator. Programs following the supper are for youth, choirs, adults, and meetings of various committees. The supper and subsequent programs have become an important part of the leadership training process and fellowship activity in the congregation. Attendance at this weekly evening session has more than doubled (to 475) during the past three years.

Outreach is a critical element in Trinity Church. Sunday

school classes are asked to focus on an outreach interest and to support at least one mission/outreach program based on their interest. Classes have chosen to support programs for abused women, Head Start, female ex-offenders, and a pregnancy life center. The pastor has a contingency outreach fund to assist those who need immediate or emergency assistance. The church supports programs for senior citizens, single parents, schooling for mentally retarded persons, and contributes to Habitat for Humanity, plus other benevolent community activities. These local outreach activities are in addition to national and world mission programs.

The church's mission programs include a budget item for national and world missions. Additional emphasis on missions is through the annual missions fair. An important part of the mission fair is the faith giving program. In this program, people pledge a certain amount just for missions. This is a faith pledge because it is over and above other giving to the church. In 1988, this program, connected with the annual missions fair to which missionaries were invited and mission activities were described, raised $35 per member for specific projects. In addition, mission trips have sent members on work projects to Haiti and Brazil within the year.

The music program, worship, and small groups—especially adult education classes for Bible study—are essential elements in the vitality of this congregation. A planning committee is working to find ways to better serve the members and the community. Helping them to discover opportunities to witness to Christ is a central task of the church's leaders and staff.

St. Paul's: Small Town

Small Town is located fifty miles west of a major Midwestern metropolitan area. An interstate highway is about seven miles north of town, but its effects have been felt in various ways by the residents since its completion ten years ago. It has made travel to larger communities for some services—especially medical and commercial—much easier and faster. For example, a trip to the hospital in the neighboring town takes fifteen minutes compared to half an hour before the interstate was constructed.

Another effect of the interstate has been the elimination of the train stop that historically connected Small Town to the world through the nearby metropolis. This loss was somewhat offset by a quicker auto trip to the airport. However, some old-timers talk with nostalgia about the train trips of yore.

The town has had spurts of growth and decline in population due to economic forces during the past three decades. Even at its zenith, the population barely reached 2,000 and now stands at 1,872. The attractiveness of the town for most of its young people remains slight. They tend to leave for work elsewhere shortly after graduation from the local high school.

St. Paul's church has had a historically limited place in this predominantly Catholic community. In keeping with its status as the largest Protestant church in town, St. Paul's has grown during the past five years from 84 members to 140 members. This has been due to a new spirit in the church, which seems to be the result of a good combination of lay and clergy leadership because relatively few new residents moved into town during this time. Average attendance at the single worship service on Sunday morning has grown to 106.

The Sunday school grew slightly to 111 members last year, and average attendance at Sunday school was reported to be 80. A slight increase in the number of young children and young parents in the community was the stimulant to growth in the Sunday school. The pastor is given much of the credit for making the church attractive to these people in the community.

The budget grew from about $550 per member to $580 per member (in 1988 dollars) during the past five years. The economics of the area have improved somewhat as a new small industry moved into town. It increased the economic base that has depended on the many workers who find jobs in the metropolitan area to the east. About 4 percent of last year's budget was sent to the denomination for benevolences.

Three important changes have affected the church within the past three years. The first was a pastoral change three years ago. This change brought a younger person into the church as pastor. This person has helped invigorate the church's leadership and has helped create a feeling of innovation.

The second change has been an increase in the number of young children and women within the past year and a half. These people are coming from the few new residents, but most are from families who have not attended any church for years.

The third change came as a result of the decision to remodel a part of the church building. This decision has sparked new interest in the church and has produced a surge of confidence in its future. Each of these changes has played a part in revitalizing the congregation.

Community outreach is limited because of the number of volunteers available to the church; it is usually done in connection with other churches in town. A FISH program was started two years ago, and a modified Meals-on-Wheels program is in operation. The church has a small emergency fund for transients and for people who have come on extremely hard times. The fund is handled by a small committee and the pastor. A regular lay visitation program for the sick and elderly is an important part of the church's own outreach program.

The mission emphasis of the church includes money sent to the denomination, but other special concerns—such as a missionary in Africa, support for hunger programs, and a missionary in Peru—are also important. The plate or loose offerings at Christmas and Easter are used to support the mission emphases of the congregation.

Church leaders are anxious to create programs to attract young people and young couples. Although relatively few of such persons live in the community, they are the expected hope for the future. In the meantime, the church has expanded its ministry with older adults, primarily because some of the church leaders are in the older age categories.

The worship experience is regarded as a high point in the life of the church. The service is based on the sermon, although considerable attention is given to fellowship needs during the announcements and prayers. Music is important even though its quality is not a point of praise among the parishioners. Special music by individuals and small groups is common at the worship service.

A key to the vitality of this church is the manner in which the leaders keep looking to improve the ministry of the church. They are interested in evangelization, Bible study, and making certain that people feel at home in the congregation. These interests have produced such a warmth and friendliness that the church need not advertise other than through the words of its members.

Good Shepherd: Downtown

This church is now on the edge of the major commercial district in the heart of a southern metropolitan city. The area around this once prestigious church has suffered urban blight for at least a decade. Various waves of new residents have swept over the nearby aging apartments and have turned them into less than desirable housing. Some commercial structures close to the church have been renovated, and a new office building has been constructed within a block of the church building.

These efforts at urban renewal have not done much to remove the blight of the general area, nor have the new and renovated buildings done much to attract permanent residents into the adjacent neighborhoods. The main influx of people is on the workday between 8:00 A.M. and 5:30 P.M.

Significant issues for church leaders have been how to minister in spite of the blight and, because of the new office building, how to function effectively with a decrease in the number of nearby parking spaces. The latter is a special problem during weekdays when programs for older persons are conducted. However, the majority of church members are committed to their church's mission and ministry and are finding ways to cope.

This formerly large membership church—at one time it claimed 2,650 members—declined to 288 members with an average attendance at worship of 117 during the past year. Ninety members were removed by death last year, which indicates a problem facing the church: its age structure is getting old.

The Sunday school, attracting children and youth from the neighborhood, had 268 members and an average attendance of 153 last year. Sunday school members tend to be young and black, while church members are older and white. The aim of church leaders is to bridge the gap between the races and to continue a ministry with the new residents of the community. Church leaders accept the need for drastic changes in their church's outlook and operation before their hopes of a truly vital church can be fully realized.

Historically the church has been active in the community. However, as the years passed and members moved away and grew older, the congregation lost touch with new community residents. The church was so absorbed in starting a new church in a growing suburb about a decade ago that its attention was directed away from the immediate community. In fact, many of the church members of the new congregation left Downtown Church to join the new church. This left the downtown church with a weakened program for at least a decade. However, during the past three years, an attitude of renewal has permeated the church, and leaders have sought once more to find avenues of service to the community.

Current outreach programs include a day-care center for community residents, involvement in refugee resettlement, and sponsorship of classes for English as a second language. It provides food, clothing, and shelter to needy persons through a fund administered by the pastor.

This congregation has been interested in missions throughout its history and has been a strong supporter of denominational mission programs at the regional, national, and world levels. In addition to sending money through the denomination, this church helps support a regional rural ministry and provides an annual scholarship for a seminary student as special mission projects.

Long-term church members are very much aware of their age and the types of community changes that have occurred around the church. They are enthusiastic about their pastoral leadership and are intent on finding and recruiting younger persons. The first fruits of their labors were evident last year as a new Sunday school class for young single adults was started. This was the first new class started in the church in more than a decade.

Bethel: County Seat

County Seat, in the heart of the nation, is a community of 9,500 persons. It is the center for the regional government in that it is the place where court is held and licenses must be purchased. It has a long history and is considered to be an attractive, conservative town. Its residents value family life. Consequently, County Seat has strong community and service institutions.

The community's economic base is varied, which keeps it fairly even during good and bad times. The age structure of the town is varied, but the community is home to relatively few ethnic groups.

Bethel Church has a good reputation that is maintained by its 365 members. On an average Sunday morning approximately 170 of its members will attend one of the two worship services. The budget (in 1988 dollars) was about $500 per member. The Sunday school had a membership of 257, of which 130 were present on a typical Sunday.

This church developed a strong adult education program three years ago, and it has been a major force in attracting young adults and young couples of the community. The basics are Bible study, but the several classes cater to age groups as well as to interests other than pure Bible study.

Outreach is basically for the needy of the community, and mission giving is primarily through the denomination. The church attempts to send 10 percent of its total budget to missions.

The worship service is considered one of the best in town. It is anchored by strong biblical preaching and is noted for having good music. For a town of its size, the number of choirs at Bethel Church (five) is thought to be exceptional.

Faith: Urban Fringe

Originally this was a small town several miles away from an urban center. However, an interstate highway was built just outside of town during the past two decades. While no immediate growth followed the highway's construction, as the years passed suburbs began reaching out along this artery. Finally, people who could afford to drive several miles to work sought out this community because of its quiet and quaint character. An inflow of new residents began about five years ago.

The citizens were not certain they wanted the town to grow and kept developers at bay for some time. Then a few people began to sell parts of their farm properties, and building started in earnest. It has grown in momentum. New residents are moving into developments around the community. The number of new homes and new people sometimes overwhelms long-term residents.

The town has a good economic base, thanks to a few small high tech service firms located around its edge. It has a good retail base because of the two malls, one on each side of the town, that draw people from several miles out in the country. In the recent past a mail order firm has moved to town. This firm provides a considerable number of jobs, especially during holiday seasons.

Faith Church was small for its first eighty years. At no time had it more than 75 members. The church building was limited in size, although it was on a lot that took most of a block in town. Parking was on the street, although an empty lot across the street was used for overflow crowds at Easter and for some funerals. The parsonage was beside the church building on part of the property.

During the past five years the congregation has grown from 73 members to the present 375. The congregation has bought a new parsonage in one of the developments and uses the former parsonage for Sunday school and fellowship meetings. A new church building with Sunday school rooms and a fellowship hall is being planned.

The pastor, who helped the congregation accept the idea

of growing, was careful in his planning. He secured a consultant to lead the church in a futuring and planning process. He assisted laypersons in creating a leadership base that included long-term as well as new church members. He worked hard on his sermons and helped laypersons design and activate a visitation program for newcomers.

A new stewardship program that included pledging was started, and church bulletins became a regular part of the service. Two adult education classes were started about three years ago, and now there are five such classes. The pastor used as many opportunities as possible to interest people in the church. The church exudes a feeling of being alive and welcomes new people into its life.

Support for missions goes primarily through the denomination, although collections are taken at Christmas and Lent for special projects. A work team for a project is being planned for next summer.

Six Churches as Types

These six churches, each having become vitally active within the past five years, are prototypes of many others. These sketches depict actual congregations that currently are facing and overcoming the most common problems besetting churches. The manner in which they have met the challenges to be in ministry and mission hold lessons for those who will listen and observe.

The characteristics of vitality displayed in each of these congregations will continue to guide the discussion in this book. The six themes need to be lifted up for review.

1. Lay member involvement, both as leaders and as participants, is very good in a vital church. The church's membership is open to new ideas and is willing to support innovation and change.

2. Worship services, including the music, are exciting at best and very useful to participate in at worst in vital congregations. Although the music may be very good or mediocre, it is an important ingredient of worship. Of particular importance are the choirs that encourage the participation of persons from all age groups.

3. Sunday school is quite important. Particularly important in the vital church with much growth is the creation of adult Christian education classes. These classes perform several functions, as will be seen, but their primary role is to help adults in the context of a supportive atmosphere find faith solutions to issues they are confronting.

4. The stewardship of a vital church, financial and voluntary, is exemplary. People give their time because they believe in what the church is doing for them and for others. They give money to support the church's programs and mission for the same reason.

5. Community outreach and missions are crucial programs in a vital church. This congregation, through its mission activities, shows members how to care for others. The pastor's messages are lived out in volunteer activities in the community by laypersons and in the nation and world through their offerings.

6. The pastor is a leader. The pastors in the example churches above represent a range of ages and races. A third of them are female. The common denominator among them is their emphasis on preaching, pastoring, and training. They help stimulate and guide laypersons, but do not attempt to control their churches' programs.

These six characteristics of vital churches are the focus of the following chapters. Each characteristic is described in detail. However, the characteristics do not live and thrive apart from one another. In vital churches, these themes of vitality interact, interweave, and are supportive of one another. And there was not a vital church in these studies that did not have all of these characteristics. In a few cases, some characteristics were more evident than the others.

We begin with lay involvement, a key factor in creating and sustaining vitality in a congregation.

II

Lay Involvement

Active involvement of laypersons as leaders takes one of three avenues in a congregation. One avenue is for a few of the laity to control the church, its ministry, and its mission. In many instances, this control is a by-product of a family tradition of being very active participants in a congregation. This type of situation is often found in smaller congregations that have extended families in the membership. In these situations one family tends to become dominant and rules on mission and ministry items out of personal desire and/or need. Quite frequently the control is unconscious, with no intent to hinder the work of the church. The primary problem is resistance to any change in the focus of ministry and mission of the congregation.

The second type of control, although done more consciously, relates to finances. This type of control takes place in congregations with one or two major givers whose contributions can make or break the budget. These persons can, and often do, decide the direction in which a church's ministry must go either by giving or withholding money. For example, the pastor and three lay leaders of a church in

Morestowne wanted to develop an outreach program, particularly to start a food bank for the needy in the community and to establish an emergency repair fund, especially for older persons who needed immediate help with housing problems. The two persons who contributed more than 68 percent of the congregation's budget did not see a need for these programs. In fact, they were adamant in their opposition to the church's sponsoring or being involved in such programs. The pastor went ahead with the projects but had to close them down within two months because of a lack of money.

The third type of control is in ministry and mission. A congregation's program depends on volunteers to do the work. In one congregation, the outreach committee voted to become a sponsor of Meals-on-Wheels. The vote was unanimous, but no one in the congregation agreed to work in the program. Although the program was ecumenical, it depended on every sponsoring church to provide six workers who would either prepare the food or deliver it. The work had to be done each day. Since this church did not respond with workers, the program was ineffective and had to be curtailed in that community. In this instance, which could have been an adult Christian education program, a Sunday school class, or any other type of program in the church, the laypersons agreed to it in principle but vetoed it by not working in ministry. This type of control may be insidious, but it is fatal to a church striving to be vital.

Lay involvement in these three types of situations meant control and resistance to new directions in ministry and mission. In these situations, the church's programs tend to be traditional and limited. The pastor cannot be innovative and creative because control is by a few influential laypersons who do not want change. This type of involvement by active lay leaders is restrictive. It limits and hinders the program and ministry of a church. It is not found in vital congregations. Lay involvement that controls finances, program, and policy was not discovered in the vital churches examined during the research underlying this book. Lay involvement in vital congregations is entirely different. It enables the church to be in mission and ministry because the laity are participants in ministry. This nonrestrictive type of lay participation is described in the remainder of this chapter.

Participants in Ministry

"Hey Bill! It's good to see you."

"Hank! It's been a while. But I've heard good things about your church! It looks like you have a runaway. What're you doing?"

"Probably the same as most others. Except we have a pretty good program for getting laypeople involved."

. "What do you mean? Everybody has to have laypeople involved."

"That's what I mean. The only thing that might be a little different is that the laypeople in our church really make the program work. They do visiting, are in charge of the evangelism program, and promote stewardship. They've also helped create a strong education program for adults that includes at least one course requiring a two-year commitment."

"Now that's something we don't have, a strong adult Christian education program. We haven't gotten around to it yet. Anyway, I don't think we could ever do a course that takes a two-year commitment. Our people don't seem like the kind to do that. But I'm curious. How did you get the two-year program started? And how do you keep it going?"

"It took a while to convince the lay leaders it was the

thing to do, but we decided it would be good for us for two reasons. First, we figure that a long-term commitment to Bible study is one way to train new leaders. Second, the Bible study is a very good method of acquainting members with the total Bible and of helping them formalize their theology."

These two pastors, as they exchange notes on their congregations, are sharing their concepts of lay involvement. For one pastor, lay involvement is much more developed than it is for the other. His congregation has a program of Christian education for adults that demands a significant commitment of time and energy. Also, the leaders in this church use a part of the adult Christian education program as a place to train new leaders. What the pastor did not say was that this church uses the two-year Bible course as a sabbatical study leave for some of its leaders.

This church has adopted a tenure system that allows a person to serve only three years as an officer or member of a committee. Following this term the person is asked to take at least one year off before being selected once more as an official leader. Several former leaders are enrolled in the two-year course for a refresher. It gives them a breather from duties while it helps stimulate their thinking. Some of these leaders view the class as one means of preparing for future leadership roles. The course serves as a time for deepening commitment as well as learning.

The pastors in this superficial conversation skirted an underlying issue related to lay involvement: the amount of responsibility laypersons ought to have in the total life of the congregation. If they had discussed this issue, the pastor whose congregation offered a two-year Bible study course for leaders could have explained how laypersons in his congregation really make the entire church function well.

They Make the Church Work

"What does it mean for laypeople to make the church work? I think they are critical to our congregation's programs, but statistics on attendance and membership suggest that they do a better job in yours."

"Making the church work means more than being elected leader of some group or committee. Our leaders lead because they have an important voice in the life and ministry of the church. I, as the pastor, help set directions and challenge them with new opportunities for ministry. But lay leaders' ideas are taken seriously, and most of the time they are put into practice because the people are turned on by them."

"What's that about the pastor's role? What do you mean by helping set directions and challenging them?"

"In my view, the pastor is primarily a pastor. That means the pastor plans and leads worship, visits, teaches, and trains. The pastor is very much involved as a church school teacher of adults. The pastor challenges and helps set directions primarily in working with committees. The pastor helps them plan and explore new directions in ministry. The pastor's main roles in committees are to keep ideas coming and to administer the program of the church, not to make the church work without help."

These pastors are describing their perceptions of how laypersons who are involved in ministry are given responsibilities for the church without trying to control its direction for personal gain or satisfaction. The pastors are aware of their own attitudes about laypersons who want "to run" the church. They have discovered that there are certain kinds of laity whose interests and convictions are quite positive and can be very helpful.

Vital congregations have many laity who are not afraid to voice opinions and are quite willing to work hard. They assume leadership because they want to be active. They want to make a difference in their own and other people's lives. They want to make the church work for the purposes of winning people to Christ and serving in his name.

This is not to say that many such laypersons are not available to most churches. The difference between vital and nonvital congregations is one of attitudes. The laypeople who are leaders in vital churches are most often turned on by their church and their role in it. In the best sense, they are positive about their church.

The primary question in a church, if the attitudes of laypersons are so important, is "How can a pastor spot these individuals?" The alternative is to find a person whose idea of making a church work is attempting to control it and limit its ministry and mission. Pastors of vital congregations look for certain characteristics in lay leaders that help assure them of positive and dedicated leadership. These characteristics are positive attitudes about life and the church, conscientiousness about the jobs they assume, and continual work at personal spiritual development. Let's examine each of these in more detail.

Their Attitude Is Positive

The first characteristic sought in lay leaders in vital churches is that they have a basic positive attitude. They are willing to listen and to change. They expect to be heard and to be taken seriously. Let's listen to a pastor describe some of them.

I used to think about half the leaders I had in a church were sort of down on things in general. They were negative. Whenever a new idea was suggested they would refuse even to consider it. They had the wet blanket out so much that the more positive people kept quiet or didn't talk much at meetings. A new idea was left for me to bring up and try to push through committee.

That's not the way it is anymore. I decided that one of the ways to change the image of the church for members in it and for those who might want to come was to select people who had a positive image of life. I made it my business to recruit those kinds of people.

At first, it was really hard to convince these people that they would make a difference. They had tried to work with the "no" generation before and had decided that they didn't want to deal with them. These positive people had better things to do than be put down in church meetings. However, one by one the new people began to agree to be leaders. My promise to them was that not only would they be heard but also I would help push the best of their ideas to become programs.

We didn't have 100 percent success during the first two years. But by the third year the balance of leadership had shifted. Our disposition in the total church had shifted and became positive. We became innovative with a few of our programs. It was like a breath of fresh air that comes into a stagnant room.

This pastor, in her descriptions of lay leaders, describes her own positive approach to ministry. A pastor must be positive in recruiting laypersons with positive attitudes. The characteristics of laypersons who are leaders are equally applicable to pastors. These pastors are positive, conscientious, and spiritual.

This pastor, in talking about her church, points out five essential elements in creating a leadership core with a positive attitude. First is the recognition that leaders who are positive produce good programs and interesting activities in the church. Second, the pastor decided on the kinds of leadership she wanted and designed a strategy of leadership recruitment to get them. She wanted leaders with positive attitudes, and she knew that she was the person who could recruit those kinds of persons. Third, the pastor, during her recruitment visits, assured potential leaders of their importance in her concept of the church. She further stressed that they would make a difference. Fourth, the pastor had a timeline that was realistic. She knew it would take at least two years to change the balance of lay power. She worked on that timetable. As a result, her leaders, after three years, had a different demeanor, and the church's image had changed drastically. It had become inviting. Fifth, the pastor modeled the kind of leader she wanted by her own attitude, by her words, and by her actions. She gave them a picture of what a positive leader could be in their church.

The leadership of a church is a combination of pastor and laypersons. The descriptions of the selection process for lay leaders is workable only when the pastor's attitude is positive.

They Are Conscientious Leaders

How do you define leaders? Are they people who try to control? Do they assume jobs that should be assigned to others? A pastor has many questions related to lay leadership. Some pastors, like the one quoted earlier in this chapter, feel that they have the training to make the church work and that laypersons are there only to support and follow them. Fortunately, this attitude is not prevalent in vital congregations. Listen to a pastor of a vital congregation.

> I define leaders as those who are committed to Christ and who want to express their commitment through work and service in the church. They will use their talents and time to assist the church in its mission, outreach, education, worship, and service ministries. They will give a number of hours per week or month to fulfilling the tasks they assume in the church.

I know that sounds pretty academic, but let me illustrate what I mean. John and Judy, not married or related to each other, are in their mid-thirties and are leaders in our church. The parents of both have been active in this church for years. John's children are in the church school. John and Judy are busy at their jobs every working day and sometimes have overtime or meetings in the evenings and on the weekend. Yet, John agreed to be chairperson of the worship committee, and Judy agreed to head up the mission committee. They tell me that they block out on their home calendars the meeting times for these groups for the entire year. They also block out any special events for which they may have responsibility.

The result of this commitment is dependable and reliable leadership for two major committees. In addition, they are active in the adult Christian education program, not as leaders but as learners. They are receiving as much as they are giving. This combination of commitment and seeking is the best illustration of good leaders I can give.

This pastor's illustration captures the composite of leadership traits discovered in research on vital congregations. Laypeople in these churches, besides having a positive attitude about themselves and their church, want to be leaders in the church for the sake of witness and service. They prepare for leadership, and they take their positions seriously. They give time to learn. They believe ministry happens when they do it through their church as well as in their private lives. When they run into major personal problems, they recognize them and try to find a way to keep the church moving ahead while they back out.

In one congregation visited during the research, an interviewee told about being very active until "my heart attack." This individual said,

I feel really bad about having to give up the mission work team, but we talked about it in our family and with the minister. Our decision was to limit outside activities to just a few things. For the church that meant going to Sunday school and worship and not being a leader. It was one of the hardest decisions we had to make, but it was necessary. Our church's mission can't afford to wait for me to get well and, besides, there are plenty of other people qualified to do those jobs. I miss working with our people in the inner-city project, but that's what we as a family have decided is best for me to do right now. Perhaps we can make a new decision in a couple of years. But for now it's an enforced sabbatical.

The pastor probably would not agree that there are "plenty of other people who could do the job," but a very good replacement was found. The church was able to continue expanding its program in mission by tapping a person who had been trained and had been serving as an alternate on the work team with the heart attack victim.

This experience suggests two additional items about lay involvement. Laypersons should be trained in tandem— that is, in groups—so that if one leader is incapacitated another will be able to assume responsibility immediately. Second, making decisions regarding lay involvement is not an individual commitment. Commitment by a layperson to lead in the church involves several people, even for single adults. The family and friends of individuals are intimately affected by a decision to become active in church leadership positions.

Leaders in vital congregations were active in ministry. They were ministering by visiting, teaching, and working in mission situations. They *did*, as well as *planned*, ministry. These leaders, in addition to being active, reported that they got more than they gave. They learned by teaching; they were witnessed to by visiting; and they were ministered to through their work in outreach. Their active ministry was a giving and receiving proposition. The reason for this was their spiritual development as Christian leaders.

50

They Are Spiritual

"I come to church to learn how to pray and follow Jesus." That simple statement of intent was expressed by a layperson who is a leader in a vital congregation in the panhandle of Texas. His perception of spirituality was trying to let God work through him regardless of where he was. In his efforts to satisfy the intent, he had started a men's prayer breakfast and organized a Bible study group. The men's Bible study group, which was mentioned by half of the people interviewed in this church, was started by Jim. He felt it would be possible to get a few of his friends to come to church if there was an informal, but purposeful, reason for them to be there.

Jim decided to become the leader of a Bible study group and invited half a dozen men to join him. The most convenient time for them to meet was early on Sunday morning. In a year, this men's Bible study group had attracted about a dozen regular attenders, half of whom did not regularly attend morning worship. This Bible study group was one man's effort to deepen his spiritual life while sharing the gospel with others.

Spirituality for another layperson was trying to serve Christ through the church's outreach to young ex-offenders. She wanted to grow in grace and felt led in this direction, although she confessed to having no experience in this ministry prior to signing up to spend one night a week with this group. She prayed about it "for quite a while before taking this step. It was frightening, but the Lord directed me on. It's been a fantastic growing and humbling experience for me." This program was not a part of her church's life until she organized it.

A key element in spiritual growth, according to laypersons in these studies, is learning to pray and finding a supportive group with which to share experiences. Bible study has afforded this opportunity in several congregations where this has become the major focus for adult Christian education. No one who spoke of the vitality of their congregation failed to mention an increased spiritual depth for themselves as well as for the congregation as a whole. Spiritual depth was the battery for their lives.

Summary

Laypersons in vital congregations do not control or limit the mission and ministry of their churches. Instead, they understand themselves as participants in God's ministry and mission through their church. They help make the church work by participating and leading in every facet of its life.

The pastor, who is the model for the attitudes and characteristics of lay leaders in vital churches, seeks persons who are positive, conscientious, and spiritually motivated to become leaders. The combination of pastor and laypersons with great interest in spreading the Word and doing the work of God among people results in a strong and vital congregation.

The emphasis on spiritual development in vital congregations has resulted in creating worship services through which personal and corporate experiences with the Holy Spirit have become quite real. In fact, the worship experience is one means of judging the vitality of spiritual depth according to interviewees in these congregations. It is to this element of vitality that we now turn.

III

Worship

It feels so good when I come into church. It feels like I really belong here. It's been like that since the first time I came for a visit three years ago. People are so warm and friendly! They welcome me so that I feel wanted. I get the feeling they think I'm important. "Spiritual" is the best way to describe the feeling. Even on my bad days, I can feel the Spirit when I come here.

Our worship service always has something of the unexpected in it. Most of the time this is because of the music, but every once in a while someone is invited to come to the front to give a testimony or say something. Don't get me wrong, we have very dignified and structured services, but there is always something special. Last week, for instance, a student from Africa was visiting, and the pastor asked him to tell a bit about himself. The young man felt moved to tell more than a bit. His speech was a mini-sermon. It helped us know more about missions. That's what I mean. The service is structured, but it's spontaneous. Somehow, it all works together.

If I had to find one thing that's outstanding about our worship it's the sermons. Our pastor bases his sermons on the Bible. They are practical and directed to where we live, I guess because he's always visiting us. To me, the sermons make the service.

Music is the key to our worship. I love music. Our people aren't very good singers, but that's all right. I can stand there and praise the Lord with my scratchy voice and no one stares. And we have special music at every service, twice in the morning and once on Sunday evening. These special music pieces may be accompanied by a guitar or a violin or an organ. It makes no difference. The music specials may be done by a group or a soloist. That doesn't matter either. The music is there for us to enjoy and participate in.

These interviewees' responses to a question about what they perceive as the strongest element in their worship experience underscores several important components of worship services in vital churches. First is the expectant atmosphere and warm tone of the congregation prior to worship. The attitude and atmosphere are maintained throughout the worship experience. The second component is the expectation people bring to worship. In vital congregations the worshipers, including visitors, believed something important was going to happen to them personally at the service. Respondents in the studies said they were seldom disappointed by the quality of the worship services in their churches. People in the studies felt their attendance at worship was their most important time for spiritual vitalization. The third component of these worship experiences was a music program. Regardless of how varied the music might be, it fit the needs of the congregation. This meant the music was as varied as the congregation. In this sense, music helped worship to be an inclusive experience. The fourth element was dynamic preaching based on biblical study. Everyone mentioned biblical preaching.

Highlighting one or more of these elements, or setting the tone and the manner in which these elements are combined in a worship service, is the responsibility of the pastor. The pastor creates the tone for worship not just on Sunday but in every formal and informal contact he or she has with the worshipers. The worship service on Sunday is a culmination of experiences for and with the pastor and reflects her or his perceptions of the needs of the worshipers.

As we examine the worship service it is well to remember that the person in charge, the pastor, must be in touch with the people and the Holy Spirit before the congregation becomes and stays vital. Vitality must be worked at in order to be achieved and maintained. One of the pastor's key roles is ensuring that worship services contribute to spiritual vitality.

Worship Is a Vital Experience

The general feeling before and during worship in a vital congregation is one of expectancy. People come to worship seeking assistance in their lives. They do not come to be observers, nor do they expect a performance by the choirs or by the worship leader.

The mood of the worshipers and leaders appeared to be a serious search for spiritual awareness. This is not the same attitude one might find in a worship service conducted by and for charismatic Christians. For example, there was no expectation of speaking in tongues or an expectation that the services would climax in a visible display of God's power. The mood was conducive to a strong sermon with personal benefits in spiritual development. (Incidentally, none of the congregations in these studies indicated it had a charismatic group within it.)

The respondents insisted that the tone in the sanctuary was worshipful from the moment they entered it until they left following the service. This included the time of fellowship as they greeted one another and the pastor as they left the sanctuary.

These reports may seem to be self-fulfilling statements with all of the definitions about spirituality and vitality being supplied by respondents in the studies. This did not prove to be the case. Visits and interviews, plus a careful reading of responses, revealed that people in vital congregations were quite specific when they identified elements contributing to the tone of worship. The major elements were the attitudes and actions of ushers, greeters, and other worshipers; the bulletins with their good news and challenges through announcements and programs; the recognition given to people, especially visitors (somehow the service was personalized no matter how large or small the number of attendees); and the general attractiveness of the sanctuary. Let's examine each of these briefly.

In the first place, the mood or tone of the service was conveyed by the ushers and greeters as people entered the sanctuary. Generally, the tone expressed by ushers and greeters was that everyone, regardless of status or garb, had equal access to God. Each person received a warm greeting. Both newcomers and regular attenders were made to feel welcome and wanted.

One difference between a vital and a not-so-vital congregation can be measured by how many people welcome newcomers and regular attenders. In a vital congregation, several people make it their business to greet others, especially visitors. It is a friendly and warm greeting, not superficial. It is not the kind of greeting reserved for the first visitor a church has had in a year. Greetings and interest in people are genuine.

The mood generated at the outset of the service by the ushers and greeters is continued during the service by the choir and worship leaders. Choir members obviously enjoy what they are doing. The music is uplifting and is an integral part of the service. The worship leader expresses warmth and concern for worshipers in all aspects of the service. The worship bulletins convey a feeling of activity and vitality within the congregation. It contains announcements about events and people, a listing of meetings, identifies opportunities for training and inspiration that are available outside this church, and lists service opportunities in which members may become involved, such as volunteer work at city missions, ecumenical food pantries, and the like. There is a combination of church, community, and world concerns in the bulletin.

Visitors are given special recognition, although they are not asked to stand and be introduced. In some congregations, a time is provided for everyone to stand and greet one another. This affords an opportunity for special greetings of visitors by pew partners. The general atmosphere of the service dictates when this recognition occurs, and it is an important part of the service. In some cases, visitors are given special name tags or ribbons to identify them for members of the church to greet.

Everyone is encouraged to sign a guest book or pew attendance pad. This is another means of identifying and recognizing visitors. In some churches, visitors are greeted by persons from at least two church organizations after worship. No visitor is recruited for leadership immediately, but descriptions of the kinds of groups and their activities may be given to people after each worship service either by an usher or a greeter. This overview of the church usually is in the form of a brochure or a folder describing the church and its programs.

Since people are singled out and given several kinds of personal invitations to participate further in the church's life, the feeling of being important and wanted is conveyed to each visitor. Doing the greeting and inviting makes the members feel especially important.

The sanctuary is well kept, nicely lighted, and in good repair. The decor is inviting and encourages worship. This, along with the human interaction from members, generates a tone of warmth and welcome for members as well as for visitors.

Small rural settings, suburban churches, county seat churches, ex-urban churches, and older downtown congregations shared in creating an inviting and warm feeling for worship. This warmth seemed natural to attenders, but it takes a great deal of work and pastoral care to create such an attitude in the church. After all, the worship service is a reflection of the general life of a congregation.

The difference between vital and nonvital congregations is quite evident in the quality of the worship experience. While a part of the quality has been discussed as creating an atmosphere in which worship occurs, two other important aspects are the music and the preaching.

Music

Music at worship ranged from very good to mediocre in terms of professionalism in vital congregations. This was the composite judgment of those who attended the services. In large and in some growing churches, the music program tended to be under the direction of trained musicians. In certain situations the choir's four sections were anchored by one or more paid professionals. The paid people were not always members of the congregation. In other settings, especially in medium and smaller-sized congregations, volunteers had complete charge of the music program. In these situations the program depended entirely on the voice quality and training of individual choir members. The degree of professionalism of the director had much to do with the quality of the choir.

An important element in vital congregations was that the choirs were growing in number. Most of the vital congregations reported that their adult choirs had increased in number as the congregation gained in vitality. A part of this change, from the perspective of those reporting, was due to an openness to new choir members that came from the warmth and friendliness found in the worship service. However, other interviewees intimated that a change had come about within the choir sometime during the past two to three years that "opened it up" to new members. An increase in choir membership appeared to be preceded by a change either in ministers or in choir directors.

In most instances when there had been growth in the number of choir members, the change was described by the interviewees as having been painful. The dynamics of choir leadership and participation evidently have effects on, or are affected by, congregational vitality. It is most probable that congregational vitality produced changes in the choirs.

Vital congregations reported starting new choirs either to reach a particular age group or to revive a musical tradition at the church that had fallen into disuse. For example, one small-membership church reported starting a youth choir that began with three members. After a year it had grown to six. This choir was considered to be an important addition to the worship program and an especially critical advance for the youth program. The individual who had started the choir was not a well trained musician but was given the responsibility because she was interested in using this method to reach the youth. She relied heavily for musical direction from the pianist who was in charge of the adult choir.

In other settings, choirs were started for younger children to supplement youth and adult choirs. In a few situations handbell choirs were begun. The latter is an expensive undertaking and generally was reported in the more affluent and larger vital congregations. In most places with handbells, there was more than one choir, such as a youth bell choir and an adult bell choir. The additional choirs were given several opportunities to assist at worship. Youth and children's choirs were regularly scheduled in worship services to supplement adult choirs. This was a bonus for most churches that had not had variety in the types of choirs that had participated in worship services. Handbell choirs often played preludes and postludes.

A second aspect of vitality through music was encouraging members of the congregation to be more active in its music ministry. For example, individuals and groups were invited to sing or play for worship. Some of the groups and solos were not very good, but the congregation generally welcomed their efforts. The quality presented by this variety was not appreciated by everyone in the congregation, but they defended the opportunity to encourage people to lead in music by those volunteering to do so. In general, the addition of groups and solos not related to the regular choral program added a dimension not often found in worship services.

A third aspect of the music program in vital churches is that it is different for each of the worship services. Most vital churches have more than one service on Sunday. They either have two services on Sunday morning or a morning and an evening service. Smaller congregations tend to have the morning and evening services, although this is not a pattern exclusive to them. At least one of the worship services is informal with special attention given to groups or solos for music. In some situations, persons who normally would not participate are encouraged to do so as soloists or as a part of a musical group.

Music in vital congregations is an important part of the worship services. It is not offered as a separate element but is integral to the intent of the service. This takes planning by the pastor and the choir director for worship and music. When these two principles have difficulty in working together, the church may not be able to provide a spiritually dynamic worship service.

More Than One Type of Service Is Offered

In most vital congregations there are multiple worship services, and one worship service is not necessarily similar to a second one. Changes in worship format are subtle and tend to reflect the leader's perceived needs of the worshipers. Even though the same worship bulletin may be used for every service, differences occur because of the emphasis in any given service by the pastor. The differences are based on the pastor's observations of the kinds of worshipers in attendance and the perceptions of their needs. Sometimes, especially when a choir or group other than the choir is scheduled for music leadership, differences in types of services are planned.

One vital congregation, when it decided to add a third worship service on Sunday morning, focused on young adults whose life-styles precluded worship later than 10:00 A.M. The pastor assigned to this service was the individual whose responsibility was young adult ministry. The eventual success of the service depended on this pastor's ability to keep in touch with the spiritual needs of those to whom he ministered. While this is an extreme example, it points out a conscious effort to identify and to try to reach a particular group through worship designed just for them.

In smaller congregations, differences in worship were found in the morning versus evening services. The evening service more often included personal testimonies, special music, and more music than did the morning service. The "regular" choir did not sing for the evening service, although a choir composed of worshipers often was recruited. The evening service often was more informal and more personally oriented than the morning service.

Another type of worship service occurred in Sunday school classes. This service was important in vital congregations. Vital congregations not only stressed the need for adult education, but they also wanted those adult classes to begin with devotions that were more than a prayer. Singing, testimony, and prayer were combined in a small group setting so these worship experiences became important adjuncts to the larger worship service of the congregation.

Sunday school classes usually had a worship leader. They used a hymnal different from the one used during church worship. They tended to be more personal in their prayers. These services were felt to be an important part of the class time.

A fourth type of service took place on Wednesday evenings. In some churches the Wednesday evening meeting was designed for fellowship followed by committee or organization meetings. It usually began with a meal after which a short service started the next phase of the evening. The service was informal but was led by the pastor, who shared concerns about which she or he was aware and a brief message that helped focus the community's attention on the meetings and study sessions yet to come. The pastor often taught a Bible study class after the meal.

Preaching Is Biblical and Outstanding

A vital congregation is grounded in a faith based on biblical preaching, especially the story of Christ's life and resurrection. Even though this was pointed to as a basic strength, when asked what they felt they needed to become more vital, respondents in these studies stressed over and over the need for a deeper understanding of the Bible. They also wanted preaching that was based on the Bible but relevant to their daily needs.

Members in these congregations usually have several opportunities to study the Bible. Adult classes tend to focus on the Bible, although they move from the Bible into daily situations for discussion during class. The Bethel Bible Series is a relatively common study device, especially for training teachers of adult classes. This background in Bible study assists the congregation in pressing the pastor for preaching that is grounded in the traditional faith .primarily expressed through the New Testament.

Few of the vital congregations described the preaching at worship merely as "adequate," nor did many praise it vigorously. Nearly all of the interviewees stated that the preaching was quite good. Preaching was the focus for the worship service and tied together its various parts. The aim of worship was to generate a feeling of the presence of the Spirit. This was directly related to the sermon. Eloquence in presenting the sermon was not desirable unless it was grounded in the faith. Yet, no one said the current pastor was the best preacher they had heard.

Summary

Critical factors in worship, according to the studies of vital churches, are the feelings of expectancy created by the atmosphere of the service; the mood of warmth and friendliness carried into the church by worshipers and continued through the service by the worship leaders; efforts to convey to all attenders that they are important; a variety of music; a time of announcements that indicate the variety and vitality of the church's mission, outreach, programs, and fellowship; and strong biblical preaching. In these vital churches, worship is the time each week when the diverse segments of the congregations have a corporate experience. The structuring of this service so that it allows people an opportunity to participate in one another's lives and encourages them to partake of the Holy Spirit is an awesome task. Such services grow out of a series of activities and shared experiences in the congregation. In one sense, worship is a culmination of other experiences and a commitment to continue together on a journey of faith.

It is important to understand that worship is an integral part of the life of a vital congregation. It is not perfunctory, nor is it a performance, although it can slip easily into a meaningless habit. The individuals in charge of the various services, including Sunday school classes, plan each to address at least one group within the congregation. This intentionality is expressed by an emphasis during the service rather than by changing the bulletin or the setting of the worship.

The elements highlighted in this chapter cannot be separated from the general demeanor of the vital congregation. There is no formula to create such an experience. It must grow out of a caring and informed group. We now turn to one aspect of creating such a congregation as we discuss the education program of vital churches.

IV

Education

Vital congregations are being affected by the trend toward a decline in the number of children and youth in the population. The children and youth sectors of the Sunday school, in general, have reflected declines in membership. The most often accepted reason for these declines is that they are due, in part, to a decrease in the number of children and youth in the families who attend the church. However, declines in Sunday school membership have been related historically to how effectively Sunday school teachers have taught. This, in turn, is a reflection of how well the teachers were being trained. Currently, as in the past, a good teacher attracts pupils.

Vital congregations understand the need for good Sunday schools. They work at it. They feel that the Sunday school is for children who come to the church. The congregations surveyed earlier made some efforts at community outreach to get people interested in Sunday school. Those efforts were limited, however. For example, none of the vital congregations had attempted to establish an extension Sunday school in a neighborhood that did not have a church. None of those interviewed used buses to pick up persons for classes or other activities. Churches that had buses used them either for youth activities or for transporting the elderly.

The training of Sunday school teachers was not done as well as some leaders would have desired in most vital congregations. As with most training programs for leaders in these churches, teachers were taught by being part of a team. This meant that they learned to teach as they taught. On the job experience was the normal pattern of training.

Pastors and lay leaders in these churches recognized the problems connected with this kind of training process. Even though they felt it was less than ideal, they saw it as necessary given the time commitments of the volunteers who wanted to teach.

In spite of this seeming criticism of the educational program, the vital churches were not weak in that area. Christian education was emphasized and was considered a strong part of the total program.

One element standing out in these vital churches was their emphasis on adult Christian education. However, this emphasis did not take away from their work with children and youth. It was aimed at work in another educational area that had become increasingly important in these churches.

The focus of this chapter is on adult Christian education programs in vital congregations. It describes an element that is in addition to strong Christian education programs for children and youth.

"Our Sunday school is pretty good, but we only have one adult class. Even so, it is the primary means we have for training our leaders. We use a Bible study all year long, but in September we have two courses. In addition to the regular Bible study class, a one-month course is given just to train our church officers."

"Our church has two adult classes. Both of these classes are for Bible study. One of the classes is led by a pretty dynamic layperson. He insists that it's Bible study, but that's just the starting point. It really deals with issues raised either by class members or by the leader during the class. I believe they deal with problems brought to the class for discussion more than anything else."

"That second class depends on having a good leader."

"You're right, but this teacher has been on target with that group. We're trying to get another class going, but we are looking for just the right leader. By the way, how did you initiate your one-month training class? Is it an effective way to train leaders?"

"I'm responsible for starting the September leadership training class. I teach it. It seemed like the best time for us to have such a class. It is on Sunday morning because we can get better attendance than on any night of the week. In answer to your second question, I believe it's effective for what we do. While we are specific about some church jobs during the class, it is used primarily to acclimate people to the purpose and the nature of the church. It helps people understand their part in making the church work. It is a required course for committee chairpersons."

"Our adult Christian education program is the means we use, probably like you, to help people become Bible literate, to ground them in the faith, and to help them think about our congregation as a place in which to find the means to put their faith to work in service. It has become a vital part of the preparation for witness and mission by our laypeople."

"That sounds more noble than what we do. Somehow, though, most of our leaders and major supporters come from our adult Christian education classes."

This conversation between two pastors underscores three reasons why adult Christian education increases the

67

vitality of a congregation. First, adults have an opportunity to attend Christian education classes with a curriculum designed especially for them. This curriculum is a mix of Bible study and topics relating to the faith needs of class members. Second, adult Christian education classes are the basis for training laypersons to be leaders. These classes also serve as an arena in which persons are recruited to become leaders. Third, adult Christian education classes provide a basis for a meaningful system of creating and nurturing small groups in the church. Because of these three functions, an adult Christian education program is mandatory for churches aiming to become or to remain vital.

Adult Christian Education as Mandatory

One of the first activities begun by any congregation is creating a Christian education program. Usually this starts with one or more classes for children. Once a congregation is large enough and has established classes for children, the next step is to organize one or more classes for youth. Educational activities for adults in many congregations tend to be limited, if present at all. In vital congregations, adult Christian education is considered to be very important. An adult Christian education program in a vital congregation features classes built on a biblical basis as well as other emphases, including witness, mission, service, and fellowship. Although the structure of an adult Christian education program and its curriculum may be similar to programs in less vital congregations, the quality and quantity of adult Christian education opportunities in vital congregations are different.

Adult Christian education in many congregations consists of one adult Bible class. This class, in various configurations, has been present in the congregation for years. It attracts at least a faithful few each week, or, in some cases, a relatively large number of people, some of whom do not attend worship. The traditional Adult Bible Study Series is used as the curriculum in several of these congregations. Such adult classes have a strong tradition within their congregations. Often, the teacher or leader has had many years of experience in teaching. He or she is respected and is quite influential in the life of the church.

While some of the leaders of such classes complain of dying loyalty among attendees and acknowledge their inability to attract new members, the class feels good about itself. Often, the respect toward a leader of an adult Bible class is reflected in the church building, particularly in large membership congregations, which may have a room named after one or more beloved leaders of this class.

Seldom does the adult Christian education program in a vital congregation consist only of a single class. The program offers more than one option. In fact, a good adult Christian education program, according to the research studies, can be a major factor in the vitalization of a congregation. Data from studies of vital congregations reveal that multifaceted adult Christian education programs are essential for three major reasons. First, they are one avenue for bringing new persons immediately into the life of the congregation. Second, these classes provide training for growth in the Christian faith for adults. Third, several of these classes become a means for establishing and maintaining a small group network in a congregation. Let's examine the implications of each of these reasons.

A. Avenue into the Life of the Church

An assumption of members and leaders in a vital congregation is that anyone who comes to worship should benefit from other aspects of the church's program. Members in these congregations feel so good about their church's program that they want others to share in it. Thus they feel that attendees at a worship service are open to evangelization. Worship attendees, especially visitors, provide an opportunity for the congregation to expand its witness.

With this feeling of wanting to share a part of a good thing in their church, members encourage visitors to attend an adult Christian education class. Many visitors—but not all—respond to the invitation and attend a class. In this way, the adult Christian education program in vital congregations is used as the entry point into friendships and into the life of the church for visitors. Also, the class is used to assist visitors in becoming involved in congregational activities other than worship.

B. Training

A second purpose for an adult Christian education program is training. Training in the adult program is two-pronged. On the one hand, training is conceived of as the primary means of assisting members in becoming Bible literate. This type of training emphasizes Bible study, ethics, church history, and missions. These aspects of training in the Christian faith are based on Bible study and interpretation of the scriptures by one or more trained teachers.

Courses and curricula for these types of adult Christian education classes may be (1) designed by an adult Christian education committee team within the congregation, (2) selected by an adult class leader, or (3) chosen by the adult Christian education committee from options offered by the denomination. No matter how the curricula are selected, the teachers must feel comfortable with them before they can be used effectively.

A second type of training accomplished in an adult Christian education program consists of preparation for church leadership. This training is done usually through short-term classes, which are designed to prepare persons for specific tasks. For example, a year-long training class for adults sequentially dealt with the subjects of trustees, finance committee, missions committee, outreach committee, education committee, and the purpose and function of deacons, elders, and stewards. Each class dealt with the purpose and functions of a specific committee as well as outlining its place within the life of the congregation. Members of the committees were expected to attend the class designed for their area of responsibility. The leader of each class was either the chairperson of the committee or the pastor.

These short-term classes were developed to prepare people to take on specific jobs in the church. The classes also were attended by some leaders who were on a "break" from a different committee, with their time off usually being mandated by a tenure rule. The "off duty" leaders felt that the short-term classes helped renew their understanding of the function of various jobs in the total life of the congregation.

C. Creating a Network of Small Groups

The third purpose of a strong adult Christian education program was to create a purposeful network of small groups. In such a network pattern, these classes served two functions. On the one hand, the class was learning about the faith and its application in their lives. The learning included instruction in disciplines such as prayer, study, service, witness, mission, and attendance at worship. The second purpose of these small groups was to be a support, fellowship, and friendship net for their members.

The notion of having small group networks is not new to congregations. However, vital congregations have given it a somewhat more useful function than merely establishing small groups. These congregations have discovered that focusing on adult Christian education is a good method for creating cohesion and long-term interest among class members. The education, fellowship, service, mission, and witness functions of an adult Christian education class in vital congregations work better in promoting an informed and cohesive membership than does using an artificial means for creating small groups, such as neighborhoods or sectors. The primary aims of networks in a vital congregation are education, service, and training in the Christian faith.

An outgrowth of adult classes in vital congregations has been an increase in service and mission activities by the church. For example, adult Christian education classes in several churches selected and supported specific missionaries in the nation and internationally. They held class fund raising events as a means of increasing the support of these missionaries. They also encouraged class members to visit the missionaries if a member was traveling in the missionary's area of work. Classes also engaged in service projects, such as volunteering to work in a community food or clothing bank. In these ways, adult Christian education classes in vital congregations added a significant stimulus to the congregation's witness, service, and mission.

Variety of Educational Offerings

Variety in adult Christian education programs in vital congregations is nearly universal. These churches work hard to have several kinds of classes, both short- and long-term, for adults. They also are more open to creating new adult Christian education classes than are less vital churches.

A combination of long- and short-term classes appears to be the norm in all sizes of vital congregations. The teachers and leaders of adult Christian education classes include the pastor and several laypersons each year. This variety of offerings and teachers was true even in churches with small memberships. In fact, smaller membership vital congregations found ways to establish variety in adult Christian educational programs by including weekday study sessions. Four patterns of programs were discovered in adult Christian education in these vital congregations.

These four patterns probably are not the only combinations of classes, but they illustrate some ways in which vital churches attempt to structure variety in their adult Christian education programs. A brief examination of each pattern is instructive.

The first pattern was to have one or more adult classes that met for most of the year. In addition to this class, a short-term special study for anyone who wanted to attend was offered at Lent or at another time during the year. The ongoing class was strong with a good leader and tended to use a Bible-based curriculum. Its members were loyal, even though some of them attended the short-term course.

The short-term course, a two- to three-month class, usually was taught by the senior pastor. This course most often was an intensive Bible study, although over the years it had included missions, social action topics, and community outreach needs. It was designed as an integral part of the program of the church.

A second pattern of adult Christian education was for a congregation to create regularly a new class for new people. New classes were created as they were needed. The length between class starts varied from a few months to two years. The point of this pattern was that new classes were planned for and expected by the church as part of its growth.

The process for creating new classes generally followed a

predictable pattern. Visitors were invited to attend existing classes. This was acceptable for a time, but established classes—like most human groups—tend to develop a life of their own. Newcomers in long-standing classes tend to feel unwanted because they have not had a significant part in creating the culture of the class.

Christian education committees in some vital congregations appear to have a policy that dictates starting a new class when existing classes reach a certain number or when it becomes obvious that newcomers are of a different age or have interests other than members of any of the existing classes. This policy has expanded the adult Christian education offerings in several of the vital congregations.

A third pattern of adult Christian education consisted of having a divided curriculum. Classes had the option of organizing as year long entities, or they could be organized as short-term—four to eight weeks in duration—to examine various topics during a year. The result of this pattern was for a congregation to have two or more classes with fixed memberships and one or more classes in which membership and attendance fluctuated. For example, one class might be a Bible study for the entire year and have the same leader throughout. A second class might discuss three different topics under the leadership of three different persons during a year. This pattern was most evident in congregations with more than two hundred attending worship service.

The fourth pattern involved having the pastor as a teacher for part of the year. This was accomplished in smaller membership churches by creating a short course of four to eight weeks as a special or additional adult Christian education opportunity. This special class was usually held during Lent. In larger membership churches the pastor was asked to create a course that could be taught as an addition to or as one of the segments of the short-term series. Both of these alternatives indicate that vital churches consider a teaching pastor to be a very important part of the adult Christian education program.

Education Includes Fellowship

Vital congregations provide good curricula and trained teachers in their adult Christian education programs. They also assume that such educational programs create opportunities for fellowship among church members to develop. Education classes form the basis for small group networks in vital congregations. These adult Christian education classes, because of their nature and purpose, offer a sense of caring for their members.

Vital congregations utilize adult Christian education classes as a means of creating a caring fellowship within the total church membership. To an outsider, the fellowship appears to occur as classes develop their own lives within the congregation. An examination of a typical sequence in the development of such a class can illustrate how fellowship and education are combined.

An adult Christian education class begins with a nucleus of three or four people. This group may have been part of a different class and decided their life or faith interests or age group dictated that it was time for them to form another class. The new class usually has a very sharp focus at its outset—such as a social action topic, a class for families with young children, recent newlyweds, or some other personal, social, or faith factor strong enough to draw the initial group together.

The new class finds, or selects from within its membership, a leader. It then asks to be sanctioned by the Christian education committee of the congregation. The class builds up on its original base by reaching out to others, often new persons in the life of the church, although the attractiveness of the topic or the type of class may be very inviting to other members of the congregation. In effect, when the class reaches out to visitors and friends of members of the class, it acts as an evangelist for the congregation. It becomes a point of entry for new persons. The class continues in this mode until it reaches an optimum size, which is determined by its ability to continue to incorporate new members effectively into its life.

This class, over time, tends to spawn another group that has a slightly different age group or interest as its primary focus. This pattern of creation continues in vital congregations. However, as new classes are started, some existing classes revise their offerings or close because they are losing too many members to continue. In any case, the atmosphere of the adult Christian education classes contributes greatly to the feeling of warmth and vitality within the church.

Fellowship is a key ingredient in the adult Christian education program. The sequence of creation, maturation, and replacement of classes is based on the ability of congregations to provide a sense of warmth and to welcome new persons and individuals. Newcomers and other members of the church who can benefit from a particular class may be brought into it by members of each of the classes. However, their interest in continuing in the class is based on their being included in the friendships and activities of the class.

Education Is An Opportunity to Be Included

Adult Christian education classes perform another critical function besides educating and providing fellowship for adults in vital congregations. This function is to open new opportunities for persons to be included in the life of the church soon after they make their first visit. This happens in three ways: The class helps people form friendships, it acquaints them with the diversity of ideas that abound among church members, and it allows people either to volunteer for leadership or to be leaders. None of these is easy to accomplish.

A. Getting Acquainted

An adult Christian education class is an excellent place for people to become acquainted with one another. This is one of the more effective ways to become introduced because the class often is organized on either common interests or age groupings. While neighbors happen to live in the same area and become acquainted by chance, Sunday school class members choose to be together. As a result they get acquainted with one another by design. This difference in the manner of becoming acquainted means a great deal in the long run. Life and faith interests tend to produce more cohesion within a congregation than do other forms of friendship. Breaking into a class for a new person, however, may be difficult even in a vital church. Groups, by nature, tend to be more exclusive than inclusive.

B. Forum for Ideas

Second, an adult Christian education class is a forum in which people can exchange ideas. It doesn't take long for a member of such a class to become aware of the variety of ideas its members hold. Exchanges between class members allow new persons and visitors to listen, to express opinions, to ask questions, and, most important, to learn. The mini-forums underscore the strength of diversities in faith and practice within the class.

Interchanges between members during an adult class session are controlled and open. Control is expressed generally by the topic, while openness is conveyed through the attitudes of the leader and the class members. Having a small group act as a forum is very important in vital congregations. Class discussions enhance the process of and the speed with which new persons become participants in the life of the church. One caution noted by some respondents was that newcomers may be hesitant to speak up and may need encouragement to participate actively in class during the first weeks.

C. Pool of Potential Leaders

Third, adult Christian education classes include as members a pool of persons who are biblically literate and interested in the church. Adult classes, therefore, become an attractive place to identify people who can be recruited as new leaders. These classes also are an ideal place for retraining and refreshing leaders who are on "sabbatical."

New persons in the church, through participation in adult Christian education classes, can test their ideas within a relatively safe environment. This testing allows them to gauge their readiness for further active participation in the church. Such testing is very important prior to their assumption of any leadership task.

An adult Christian education class can be an essential part of a training process for new persons and for other church leaders. It is in these classes that seeds and strategy for change may be born. Those seeds and strategies then can be brought forth for discussion and action by the congregation through leaders recruited from the classes.

Because adult Christian education classes provide the basis for a functional network of small groups in the congregation, leaders can be discovered relatively easily. For instance, a member of one adult class might be interested in becoming active in a certain phase of the church's life. This interest can be expressed to the class leader, who, in the normal training and fellowship events for adult class leaders within the church, alerts the person responsible for that area. The class leader may also contact the pastor to indicate interests that a member may have expressed in becoming more active in specific parts of the church's life.

Summary

Adult Christian education is a program of enrichment, mission, education, fellowship, and outreach for vital congregations. The church's programs depend on leaders who are discovered and trained through special adult Christian education classes. One of the unintended results of such a program is the creation of a network of caring small groups as well as groups built around faith and life issues. Such a program is crucial in most vital congregations because it enhances an attitude that change is both important and healthy. The program is successful only in those congregations willing to expend much energy in assisting people to integrate into existing or create new classes and to become active participants in their classes.

V

Stewardship

This entire book is about stewardship. It describes the tremendous amounts of time and energy laypersons give to and through the church to accomplish its ministry and mission. Lay leaders in many churches often give ten, twenty, or more hours each month to fulfill their duties. These hours are donated willingly. Laypersons who see something being done, in part because of their efforts, become excited about working for the church.

The chapters describing lay leadership, education, and reaching out are examples of time stewardship by laypersons in vital churches. Laypersons in these congregations are turned on by their church's program and want to make certain that it excites others. They want their church to fulfill its purpose. They want their church's ministry and mission to be meaningful to them and to others. Vital churches, because of the time stewardship of their members, are better able than nonvital churches to assist laypersons in expressing their commitment.

Vital churches use training, Bible study, mission projects, outreach activities, fellowship, and a strong tenure rule (to rotate leaders) as means for helping laypersons express their commitment. These have been (or will be) described in detail in other chapters. This chapter builds on such lay commitment from the perspective of their service and financial support of their church.

"Our church amazes me. It seems to have enough money to do anything it wants to do."

"I can't believe that. No church has enough money to do all it has to do in mission and ministry."

"You're right; except we don't attempt to do everything. We try to have a definite focus to be more effective in what we think we can do. We have goals for service and mission. Our aim in these goals is to stretch our minds and imaginations. Perhaps they aren't large enough yet, but they're big for us. And we try to meet those goals every year. So far, we have met them the past three years. These goals cost a lot of money, but money seems always to be there when we need it."

"Your goals are too modest. A church just can't have enough money."

"Maybe you're right. Our goals may be too modest. In 1988 we had 146 members with an average attendance of 123. Our budget was $148,000. In addition, each of the three adult classes supported a missionary, the collections at Christmas, Lent, and Easter went to denominational mission work in the inner city, and our people helped operate an ecumenical organization working on housing for the poor in the inner city. We have just approved an additional building project that will cost $40,000, and most of that has been pledged."

"Those figures aren't too shabby. How do you do it?"

"Simple. We emphasize stewardship and giving. Our teaching theme is that we are stewards of everything we have and that we ought to use as much as possible for the growth of God's influence on the world. That includes giving and service by every member and attender of our church."

What seems simple to this layperson from a vital congregation is not really the case for most congregations. The key element, however, emphasizing stewardship is an important ingredient in every vital congregation that was studied. However, stewardship was not played as a separate theme in this or any other vital church. As a program emphasis, stewardship was woven into the total life of the church and was so natural a part of it that relatively few persons pointed it out for special recognition. The truth was that people in these churches were so turned on by the gospel message that they gave money and time as expressions of their discipleship.

Giving Is a Part of Discipleship

Discipleship is the norm in vital congregations. By discipleship these churches mean regular practice of the disciplines of prayer, worship, learning, service, and giving. The entire atmosphere of these churches encourages members to give money, time, and possessions as means of witnessing to God's presence in life. Volunteers are recruited to participate in church programs and are sought to work in programs supported in part by the congregation, but are not for the church itself—such as at a food bank, a job counseling center, or a clothing distribution center. In the same manner, money is collected to give to others as well as to support the program of the congregation.

It is important to understand an underlying attitude about stewardship in vital churches. This attitude is directed outward, service-oriented, and giving in nature. It permeates the life of the congregation and is a motivator for various kinds of outreach and involvement by members. This discipleship attitude is based on a common conviction among members and professional staff that the church is of God and should express God's love and care toward others regardless of their stations in life. The Bible is an important guide for these people as they seek to understand God's love through the messages of Christ. Prayer is a primary means for keeping the lines of communication between God and church members open and functioning. It comes as no surprise, given their attitudes and the kinds of expectations about Christian living it produces, that people conceive of discipleship as a dynamic venture in witnessing to Christ's saving grace for them.

This discipleship attitude, based strongly on prayer and Bible study, produces general acceptance of the need for good stewardship habits. Stewardship, in the context of vital congregations, is a living out of discipleship demands. The impetus for stewardship as being a normal part of discipleship comes from the professional staff as well as from the lay leaders. It is assumed as an attitude, but the feelings about stewardship and discipleship do not exclude stewardship as an emphasis either educationally or as a financial program.

The overall stewardship program of vital congregations includes a financial campaign for pledges, usually in the fall, to underwrite the next year's budget. In most of the vital churches studied, stewardship and financial campaign materials, as well as pledge cards, were sent by mail. In larger membership churches, additional activities—such as dinners and cluster meetings—were used to explain the program and the budget. The collection of pledge cards or commitments usually was done at worship services, although home visits of one kind or another were common. The collection process often requested that persons lay their pledge cards on the altar. Putting pledge cards on the altar was more than symbolic. It was an act of worship and dedication for members of the churches using this tactic. No one discussed a stewardship program apart from the normal program of the church. It was integral. It was assumed that members would be excited about and respond to the mission and ministry of the church by giving to support them. At least one sermon about the church's program needs and stewardship was preached during the financial campaign.

Extra Mile Giving

Extra mile giving consists of contributions in addition to paying the pledged amounts to the church budget. Pledges include funds for the operating budget as well as a building or mortgage fund. Additional monies given to the church because of specific appeals are considered extra in the sense of not being within the original pledges of the members.

A church leader in a vital congregation discussed giving by members in addition to the amount of their pledge as "opportunity giving." This church provided several additional opportunities for members to give to programs, either those partially supported by the congregation or programs supported through the denomination, that would expand its mission and ministry. Some of these additional opportunities included direct support of one or more missionaries as well as support for specific outreach projects, some ecumenical in nature, in the community.

The point of "second mile" giving, from the perspective of leaders in vital congregations, was to expand the vision and service of the congregation. A secondary emphasis was to encourage individual members to become personally involved in mission.

Generating a spirit in which extra giving is more the norm

than an oddity is a trait of vital congregations. Lay leaders and professional staff in these churches choose carefully between many options for mission and service projects in which their members might be involved and that they may be interested in supporting financially. In most instances when special churchwide projects need additional funding, the extra giving is begun because someone in the congregation has had a personal experience with a receiving agency or group.

In one small-membership congregation, for example, a pastor's wife began a "March for Hunger" as part of the worship service each month. During this march, attendees at worship would bring money they had saved during the month to lay on the altar. These gifts were in addition to their commitments (this church did not use pledge cards). This money was used for hunger related projects in the community and, through the denomination, in the world. The march became a part of the life of the congregation, as did an emphasis on dealing with hunger. Related projects included opening a food bank and establishing an emergency cash fund for needy persons.

In a large-membership congregation, the senior pastor had visited a mission site in another part of the world and had been appalled by the people's suffering, caused by famine. He appealed to his congregation for money, and within about five years that church was sending both money (about $100,000 above the budget in 1988 dollars) and volunteers to the area for mission work. These volunteers decided that their expertise could best be used in educational and agricultural development. They took appropriate materials and equipment to the country to help solve the longer term problems the people faced. In addition to contributing money and time, these volunteers paid their own way, or other members of the church paid it for them, as a part of their personal special gift for missions.

As one woman said, "I couldn't go, but I made certain two others had the money to get there."

In both of these instances, not unusual among vital churches, the congregation responded to personal suggestions from church members or a pastor about projects and needs for extra gifts. In fact, this same phenomenon occurred in each of the vital churches studied. In some instances, the churches used extra gifts to support seminary students, while in others they gave to support missionaries (both inside and outside the United States). None of this extra money, however, was understood to include time and gifts given to operating or assisting with food banks, job placement offices, clothing, and emergency grants within the local community.

Extra giving added a substantial amount to the budgets of these vital churches over and above any pledged or committed amounts they received. Part of the reason for this kind of stewardship may be traced to the manner in which the budget was designed. The budget was only partially unified. Several opportunities existed for persons who wanted to contribute to areas or programs of special interest to them.

Unified Budgets

The concept of a unified budget for churches began several years ago as an effort to be responsible with the various funds a church receives. A unified budget combines each aspect of the church's program—that is, administration, education, mission, and outreach—into what is known as a program budget. In most churches, the unified budget includes mortgage payments or a building fund, plus denominational askings. In every respect, a unified budget is a rationalized way to control expenses. The unified budget is not a challenge in terms of isolating

specific programs or needs that people can underwrite directly.
Vital congregations use unified budgets up to a point. The leadership of these churches feel it is essential to have a single budget in order to be responsible both to their congregation and to the mission and ministry the members are supporting. Having a budget that encompasses most aspects of the church's program and outreach makes securing pledges or commitments easier. It also allows the congregation to monitor the percentage of money given to each program.

Several vital churches continue to promote a building or mortgage fund that is distinct from the program budget. In most of these congregations, the building fund is a separate budget, and pledging or the making of commitments is done on a card separate from the program pledge card. In most instances where this occurs, the building fund is for a limited duration, usually three years, and is for the purpose of greatly reducing or eliminating a loan or mortgage or adding to or remodeling a church facility.

In most vital congregations, an item for buildings—including mortgage payments, renovations, and upkeep—is a part of the unified budget. While it is in the budget as one of several items, some churches have pledge cards that allow members the opportunity to designate a part of their gift specifically for the building fund. This somewhat compromises the unified budget because it permits people to apportion their pledges between program and building. The leaders of congregations with such a split in budgeting reported no problems in meeting either budget.

The unified budget is modified in other vital churches when the budget lists benevolences as a separate item on the pledge or commitment cards. This may be a third choice on the card and, by providing this option, moves the church as near to designated giving as most congregations wish to be. Unless there is a congregational policy—such as 10 percent for building and 25 percent for benevolences/mission—members are completely free to choose how much to give to each portion of the budget. Relatively few churches are willing to move this far toward designated giving, although those congregations allowing such freedom believe it helps increase the amount given to outreach by their members.

Vital churches appear to be able to offer these alternative approaches to the unified budget and still meet each part of the budget. The primary reason for this ability to retain freedom and at the same time meet budget requirements stems from an atmosphere of stewardship responsibility within the congregation. The sense of stewardship appears to grow precisely because of the freedom members have to choose how much support they want to give to specific budget items while understanding the need for a balance in the mission and ministry activities of the congregation.

In short, stewardship as a means of fulfilling the discipleship demands placed upon members in a vital congregation allows the church to expand its ministry and mission by giving members options for their pledging dollars. The unstated conviction of leaders in these congregations is that the options encourage people to give more than they would if the options were not available. Perhaps that is one of the reasons pastors and lay leaders in vital congregations regularly introduce additional opportunities for extra giving.

Specific Extras Introduced Regularly

An interesting aspect of stewardship in vital congregations is the regularity with which opportunities for extra giving are presented to the membership. Some of these opportunities are based on denominational appeals—such as hunger, new church development, support for particular projects, and natural disasters. Other opportunities are decided on as "extra mile" goals by a committee and the governing body of the church. The appeals are selectively presented to the congregation primarily on the basis of the priorities of the congregation's outreach program.

Vital churches know that they cannot deal with every appeal that comes to them. They know, also, that they do not have enough resources to work effectively in every kind of need in their community. Thus they are quite intentional about the appeals selected from among the many that are asking for support by denominational and nondenominational groups as well as the church's own committees and governing body.

Many vital congregations include a few denominational appeals as a part of the unified budget, such as an ongoing emphasis on hunger or continuing support for a regional urban ministry project. These appeals become an integral part of the outreach or mission budget and require no extra funds or additional appeals.

Appeals for extra monies are generated because of projects the church leadership feels the membership ought to undertake. A few projects are supported because of a particular interest in them by the pastor or lay leaders. These may have been discovered during travel or presentations at a regional mission or outreach school. It is more likely that projects supported by the congregation grow out of needs the leadership feels ought to be met either in the community or in other parts of the world. In this sense, the church initiates outreach programs in particular areas or among specific groups.

For example, one congregation began to notice an increase in the number of young adults visiting its worship services. This church had no program for young adults but watched this group carefully. After a few months the influx continued and church leaders began to question seriously how it might be more intentional about ministry to this group. A seminary student was hired to assist in a study of options for ministry. A report of the findings was presented to the church council, suggesting the need for a more organized approach to this particular segment of incoming population in the community. The congregation's board approved the creation of such a ministry but insisted that it's support be an extra income item for the first year. The members responded by raising the money within a month, and a ministry to young adults was started. After three years the program was well established, and its support became a part of the regular budget.

A small-membership church in the inner city was continually aware of the tremendous need in its neighborhood for a food and clothing distribution center. The church's lay leaders and the pastor decided they would ask members to contribute food and clothing one Sunday each month for persons who needed them. The response was quite good for the congregation's size. The fellowship hall, the only large room in the building, became the collection and distribution center for the supplies being donated.

Soon, the pastor and two lay leaders were meeting with other churches to describe the project. Their presentation included pleas for assistance. This small congregation, which began its program with extra collections of food and clothing, became the focal point for a major witness and ministry in the inner city. The people of the church, most of whom were poor, demonstrated a vision of care and concern that eventuated in opportunities for other congregations to assist people in need who lived in the community.

Extra giving, as this latter illustration suggests, does not always need to be money. It can be in the form of commodities like food or donations to clothing centers, or it can be in the form of volunteers. Indeed, volunteers doing mission work were an important part of every vital congregation's stewardship program.

Every vital congregation reported sending some of its people as volunteers to other places where they gave their time either in work projects or in outreach programs. Some congregations, for example, sent volunteers as well as money to the small urban church described above to assist with collecting, storing, and distributing food and clothing. In the most recent year, that small church, as the focal point of a network of concerned congregations, was able to provide food and clothing to about 50,000 people.

The pastors and lay leaders of vital congregations are not willing to allow their members to become smug about giving. For this reason, vital churches continually present to their members additional opportunities for mission and ministry. Leaders in these churches believe that members need to be aware of the large number of ways in which they can contribute to God's mission.

Appeals for Missions and New Ministries

A more complicated type of appeal for additional monies occurs in vital churches that focus on a particular mission or ministry. These new foci are carefully considered and researched prior to any proposal to a church council. Most of the new projects are envisioned as lasting a considerable time and are expected to consume much money. An illustration of what occurred in one large-membership church outlines the process used by congregations of all sizes that decide to begin a new ministry.

The congregation decided that its ministry to youth needed to be expanded. The church council had some of its members look at the community, particularly the area near the church building, to determine how many youths lived there. This subcommittee reported that enough youths were in the area and not affiliated with any congregation for this church to increase its ministry to them. The council had another subcommittee look at the ways in which expansion might occur.

The decisions of the subcommittee included adding space in which the youths might have overnight events and a place away from the other activities in the church. Based on a choice among several options, the church built a wing to its existing fellowship hall and especially designed it for the youth and hired a full-time youth minister.

While this particular option is available to very few churches, the process this congregation used to decide on its approach to a new ministry can be used by churches of all membership sizes. The lay leaders and pastor of vital churches were sensitive to changes in the make up of the population surrounding the church as well as the program needs of the congregation. This sensitivity alerted the leaders to changes needed in the program to better serve particular groups in the community. A careful examination of existing and collected data was completed and recommendations for action were given to the governing body of the church. The governing body made a decision about the program, including use of space, leadership, and funding.

This process is only as good as the financial base of the church allows it to be. Without a strong and integral stewardship emphasis, vital churches would not be able to implement new ministries or missions. Yet, the challenge of new mission and ministry opportunities is continually before vital congregations. Like the large church that was expanding its youth program, vital churches find the money to do what they feel they should do. Stewardship is so much a part of the members' lives that they support expansions of ministry after the church council follows the kind of research, planning, and action process outlined above.

Summary

Stewardship in vital churches includes the careful use of time and money. Giving of both through the church in service and mission is very important. In fact, a discussion of money or time separate from each other is not acceptable to members and leaders of vital churches.

Stewardship and mission are almost synonymous to leaders of vital congregations. This discussion of stewardship underscores the need to understand better what mission means to vital churches. We turn next to mission.

VI

Reaching Out

The interview has proceeded well. The pastor has been helpful, and the laypersons have expressed much excitement about the church's program. The lay leaders and the members evidently support the pastor in her leadership efforts. The next questions, however, are a key to discovering the overall vitality of the church. The response to these questions are basic indicators of vitality according to findings from previous studies.

"What is the importance of mission to the world in the congregation? What kinds of community outreach does this church support?"

The pastor nods and grins a bit. "I'll take the last question first. We are involved in community outreach in two ways. First, we give money to two ecumenical agencies and a couple of church-related groups that are quite active in the community. Second, people from this church volunteer time to assist in church-related, mostly ecumenical, agencies—such as the food bank, the job center, and the clothing center. A few also work in the Meals-on-Wheels program. In addition, a small fund is maintained for use in emergency situations. The fund is called the pastor's discretionary account, but it is administered by two laypersons in consultation with the pastor."

"How about world mission?"

"Again, we are involved in several ways. We give through the denomination. In fact, our mission giving to the denomination is the highest per capita of any church in the conference. Also, we give directly toward the support of three missionaries, two of whom have visited our church during the past five years. We sponsor one youth and one adult work camp each year. Maybe these won't count as mission since they are in this country, but we feel that they are part of our mission program and that they are not in our community."

This litany of involvement and support for outreach and mission was bolstered by a financial report showing the amount of money given to various outreach and mission activities, plus an estimate of the number of persons involved in several church-related outreach agencies in the community.

"Our goal this year is to spend one-fourth of our budget for outreach ministries. This is not the amount I hope we will remain at, but it is our goal for the year. Within five years we are aiming for 40 to 50 percent of our budget to go for others."

"Why?"

"Because I believe the church must minister to others. If it focuses its attention exclusively on its own members, it will die. The church is an expression of God's will in the world. It must be concerned about others first and foremost."

This pastor represents the feeling of most leaders in vital congregations. Their strongest conviction is that their local church must encourage members to be involved in outreach activities within the communities in which they live and to support missions in areas beyond the local community. This twin thrust, aimed at spreading God's good news, is grounded in the understanding of Christ's message that they must go into all the world. Missions, local and worldwide, are as important to these vital congregations as are education and worship.

Mission: A Critical Factor in Vitality

An interesting phenomenon in vital congregations is the amount of time given to encouraging members to become involved in outreach and mission. In several of these vital churches, appeals for assistance—monetary and volunteer time—were made during worship services at least monthly. These appeals were as diverse as announcing the availability of sign-up sheets for a work camp being held in a particular place in a nearby city or neighborhood or in another state, introducing a student from a local college who needed a job or financial assistance in order to remain in school, or promoting a church emphasis on hunger or housing the homeless. In each situation, members were invited to be involved through either money or time. The mission emphasis included the invitation to learn more about the people for whom the money or time would be spent.

Literature promoting and explaining specific outreach opportunities and missions was available in liberal quantities in various spots in vital churches. Racks near the sanctuary, by the church office, and in the church school area were normal locations for such literature. In smaller church buildings, literature was available on a table near the office or at the rear of the sanctuary. Literature about a specific outreach need was included in the weekly bulletin in many of these churches.

One type of literature typically consists of brochures describing a particular community outreach ministry—such as the local food center, Meals-on-Wheels, or other similar activities. A telephone number, as well as an address, was included in the literature to encourage personal contacts and private donations.

A second type of literature included copies of letters from missionaries who were being supported by donations from the church. Advertisements for special events being planned at a nearby community outreach center—such as a special collection to buy building supplies for a local Habitat for Humanity project—and news stories from local papers or reprints from other places about one of the mission or outreach agencies supported by the congregation were also included.

A third type of literature was denominational or ecumenical in nature. It described a place, a need, and what the church was doing to meet that need. Contributions were asked for, with the money to go to the project through the local church.

In some vital churches a tradition has developed around work teams. The work team, as a mission enterprise, may be part of an ecumenical or denominational effort that focuses on a particular country or mission every year. Recruitment of volunteers and collection of money for their support entails informative sessions during which church members learn about the needs and what is to be done during the work team's time in the field.

These informational meetings are open to the entire church membership and precede recruitment. The typical format for the session may include time for potential volunteers to sign up at the conclusion of the final session. Some type of screening of volunteers is done by a committee in the church before the personnel of the work team is finalized. Money for travel expenses and supplies for the project team are furnished by contributions from church members who respond to a special appeal. Following their return from the project, the work team is invited to a dinner for the congregation, at which they tell of their experiences and the needs they did not have the time or energy to fill. In effect, this reporting session becomes the basis for educating members and beginning the recruitment process for a new work team for next year or for the next project.

In these three ways—direct appeals to support someone or some project, literature about specific projects and agencies, and personal involvement through volunteer experiences in mission activities—vital congregations keep mission and outreach before their members. Leaders in these churches are biased toward expressing mission through active involvement of church members. They like to see members volunteer a block of time to specific mission or outreach activities. Also, leaders tend not to be content to include missions only as an item in the budget, although that is done. Leaders in vital churches try to convince their members that mission and outreach are ways they can grow in faith and grace through personal involvement.

Members Encouraged to Be Involved in Community

Several of the vital congregations in which leaders were interviewed were instrumental in initiating community outreach programs. These programs include food and clothing banks, job or employment reference centers, referral centers for people needing a place to live, child and women abuse clinics, community health screening programs, and Habitat for Humanity. In most cases, these community-oriented programs were ecumenical both in support and in what they intended to do. Volunteers were recruited from several churches. People who used these services were not asked about their church or religious background.

Two kinds of outreach programs were nearly universal: food and clothing banks. Other kinds of community outreach varied with the needs of the community and the interests of church leaders. In most settings, leaders of vital congregations tried to focus on a few things they felt were most important in their community and toward which their church could give most assistance. This concentration usually was based on the interests of the pastor or a group of lay leaders in the church. While the interviewees admitted to being subjective in choosing the projects they promoted, the leaders pointed out that church members were encouraged to volunteer in other agencies and activities ministering to the needy in the community.

An interesting emphasis in vital churches was the feeling among some leaders and the pastor that their people ought to be involved in outreach through leadership in community agencies. In some situations this meant running for political office, and in others it was being a witness by giving leadership to special charitable drives in the community. The rationale behind these types of involvement is that a Christian has an obligation to help shape a community's life as well as to assist those who are needy. It is clear that this emphasis may have been an after-the-fact form of witness—that is, people were elected or chosen for reasons different from their own interest in furthering the church's outreach in the community. However, the concept of utilizing their position as a means of witness was important. The conviction of the churchs' leadership that witness should be integral to one's position in life generated an expectation within their members who were community leaders that their leadership positions allowed them an opportunity to speak out in the name of the church.

Another form of outreach in the community was the

beginning of attempts by some vital churches to start church schools as outposts in other neighborhoods. Church school classes, as has been discussed, are very important to vital congregations. In a few of the vital churches leaders decided that their churches were not reaching certain community residents because of either the church's location or a perception among the residents that they "would be out of place" in the building. The churches were beginning to respond by finding a building in the area where the residents lived and shopped in order to set up a church school.

While the emphasis on starting church schools was relatively recent, a couple of efforts were starting to produce results. The new church schools were relatively small, but they provided a witness to the community and thereby demonstrated that the church was interested in the people. The hope behind starting these church schools was that the church could create an entré into a previously unreachable group of people. These churches wanted to set up a center for service as well as Christian education where they had not had a ministry previously.

Another form of outreach was assisting in starting new congregations. Most of the efforts in this direction were made by large-membership congregations. However, in at least one situation a small-membership multi-racial church decided to assist in starting a new ethnic/racial church. It gave some money to rent a building, and one of its members became the lay preacher. The fledgling congregation was eventually supported by the denomination as a new church. It was initiated by a vital church that saw a need and helped to make a new church a reality.

Involvement in the community is a hallmark of vital churches. This involvement finds various ways of expressing itself so that, as one keeps following leads, a network of people and money is created to help work at solving

101

community problems as well as meeting human needs. The attitude of these churches is that God expects disciples to work with others. Witnessing through service is a normal part of ministry as taught in these churches.

World Mission Is Important

Local community outreach is expected, but world mission—that is, anything beyond the local community—is also considered to be very important by vital congregations. Emphasis on world hunger is especially appealing and is a part of many of the mission programs in these churches. Special initiatives to assist with alleviating hunger include visits by members of some vital churches who then report back on what is being done and what needs to be accomplished.

Special world mission projects were more often the rule than the exception in vital congregations. For example, a congregation supported an annual work team to construct housing for poor persons in a section of Texas along the Rio Grande. This construction crew was recruited from among church members, who were asked to volunteer ten days of their time. Building materials and construction oversight for the project were donated by a builder who was a member of the congregation. The church supported the work crew by paying for travel and lodging during their construction time.

This kind of project, although not always to the extent or the type of work done, was repeated in most vital churches. In smaller-membership vital churches, work teams were recruited from among several other congregations, and a combined effort was made to participate in such projects. Often the projects were in other countries that had been chosen by the church leaders either because they knew of a need or because they knew leaders in those areas.

In some instances, mission projects are chosen because they are part of a denominational emphasis. A congregation might choose as a partner a church in another country or in a different part of this nation. This church partner would receive support and, possibly, visits from members of the sending church. The idea is to create a personal tie between the two congregations. The "have" church shares some of its resources and leadership with the "have not" church. Very soon the sending church discovers that a rich set of resources is available to them from the receiving church. This may result in the sending church's raising money to bring a small delegation from the receiving church for a visit to this nation or church. This strengthens the personal relationships and encourages a new understanding of the world nature of the Christian church.

Projects other than work teams may focus on a special interest of the church, such as adult literacy, agricultural economics and training, or health services. The vital congregation may have several persons who are skilled in a particular occupation and want the church to support their counterparts in other places. This can be done relatively easily by using their own contacts or denominational contacts. The persons who serve as contacts allow vital churches to find entries into networks of Christians in other places who can become a focus for support and exchange.

One of the discoveries vital churches make is that their emphasis on world mission creates a large amount of personal contact with people in other places. Persons from many vital churches travel either on vacation or on business to all parts of the world. These travelers are used occasionally as emissaries of the vital church to members of churches in other places. This provides the vital church with a personalized account of what is happening and who is being helped. It also provides an opportunity for the vital church to receive feedback and information from those it seeks to support. They can talk personally with the church through the returned traveler or, as has happened in a few instances, through a video tape made by the traveler. A world mission emphasis stretches the minds and spirits of members of vital churches. They can begin to revise stereotypes and learn to know persons and churches in other places. This learning helps members of vital churches to be more receptive to the need for support systems for Christians the world over. The benefits to their church are often mentioned, although never used, as the primary reason for a world mission emphasis by leaders of vital churches.

Mission Retreat

Vital churches with a strong mission emphasis use adult education classes to teach about the need for witness worldwide. However, these churches rely on annual mission fairs or retreats to focus attention on those projects of world mission they want church members to support well. The retreat or fair usually includes a dinner on Friday and Saturday evenings, with programs on Saturday afternoon and Sunday morning. Of course, there is a speaker at each of the lunch and dinner meetings.

The purpose of a mission fair/retreat is to bring missionaries and church members into a setting in which personal relationships can be enhanced. It is here that members get to meet and ask questions of persons who represent mission agencies the local church supports or may desire to support. Vital congregations that sponsored such events had positive remarks about the quality of the interaction between missionaries and members. This positivism revolved around getting acquainted, hearing firsthand stories about the work the church was support-ing, and having a chance to ask questions about the work being done by missionaries.

Mission fairs do not just feature persons supported by the congregation. At such events, potential new projects or agencies are introduced to church members. The purpose of having representatives of agencies not yet supported is to keep church members learning about different missions and to allow them to be able to choose additional projects to support.

Although the members of the church's mission committee select certain of the mission projects for churchwide support, they may select a particular project for private support. For example, at the mission fair, members may learn about a scholarship program at a college or university that can be increased through private donations. These scholarship programs may be for minorities or for students from a particular country. It is conceivable, and likely, that the opportunity for privately funding one or more students through a scholarship will appeal to attendees at a mission fair. Those who are interested are urged to contact the person or agency for follow-up.

Thus the mission fair, with its purpose to encourage people to get to know one another, can have other effects that result in an increase in the emphasis on world mission in the lives of individual church members. This is always of interest to a vital church, and it is an expectation that is met more often than not.

Faith Promise Giving

Faith promise giving appears to be a means used by some vital churches to allow people to give to missions over and above their regular church pledge. It is used exclusively for missions.

This method of committing an amount to give on faith is done on an annual basis. It occurs in the Sunday morning worship service of the mission fair as a culmination of the activities and displays of that event. People are encouraged to make a promise—not a pledge—to give a certain amount of money, according to their determination, toward a project or a fund that supports several designated projects. This promise is not binding and is over and above the amount of their regular church pledge. The idea is for them to promise an amount that they will be able to contribute during the next year but is not available to them at the time. In faith, they make their promise.

Reports from churches using this method indicate an increasing amount of money available for missions. It appears that people do find the money, even in economically depressed situations, to meet their self-imposed faith promise. In fact, the amount promised increased each succeeding year it was used in vital churches. Part of the reason it increased is that more people were convinced that this was an important way to add to their stewardship. Another part of the reason is it appeared to help people deepen their faith. After all, when they made their promise they had no idea how they would find the money to fulfill the promise.

Summary

Mission and outreach are very important to vital churches because their leaders believe that reaching out is (1) a biblical imperative, (2) a means for helping people understand their role in witnessing to God's love and care in the world, (3) a vehicle for helping people use their talents and time in the work of the church beyond the local congregation, and (4) an opportunity to meet people of other cultures and backgrounds whose Christian commitment is as deep as their own. Educational tools are used to assist members in becoming aware of needs, and special procedures for giving encouragement to members to follow up their intentions with actions.

The key to this emphasis is the leadership of the pastor. In fact, the pastor's leadership is important in most everything done within a vital congregation. It is now time to look more closely at the pastor and the pastor's role in helping churches become and remain vital.

VII

The Pastor

"How important is the pastor? I will answer that with another question. How important is oxygen to your body?"

"Are you saying that the pastor is what makes a vital church?"

"No. Not exactly. I'm saying that a pastor is the critical element in the mix of a vital church. He or she isn't a stand-alone. But without the right kind of pastor, a congregation won't become vital."

"I suppose you have some ideas about the 'right kind' of pastor?"

"Yes. But pastors don't have to be superpersons. They are normal people with extraordinary commitments. In fact, there are two things that separate a pastor who's ordinary from one who can make a church vital. The first is commitment to Jesus Christ, and the second is enabling people to be in mission in the name of Jesus Christ."

"Let's make an assumption about the first."

"Hold on! That's the one requirement I don't make any assumptions about. I want a pastor who is committed to

Jesus Christ. A lot of pastors give lip service to the ideal, but it's the ones who are really committed that make a difference."

"I agree with that, but that would be true of most pastors."

"I would like to believe that, but we had three before this one who didn't display strong commitment to Jesus Christ. I'm sorry to have to say that, but that is our experience. Too many pastors are committed to their own careers or moving to another church setting where their talents might be better used. It's the ones who are excited about doing the Lord's business where they are stationed who are vibrant and have their churches moving toward vitality."

"I'll have to think about some of the things you've said."

"Maybe I've overstated it, but disinterest in doing the Lord's work, laziness, and being occupied with other interests are common among too many pastors."

"Much of what you say rings true. How about the second thing you mentioned, enabling others to be in mission. What exactly does that mean?"

"Look at the logistics of a church. It is located in a place where people live. Let's assume that a person, any person, can relate well to fewer than 50 people, although, on a more superficial manner, this person may interact with hundreds of others. Ministry, to be exciting and soul grabbing, is initiated best in small groups of two to five people. How can pastors in communities of more than 100 people work effectively in ministry? They can't—unless they have others to help them! Laypeople have to be motivated to be ministers if the church is going to mean anything to them or to the community in which they live."

"I'm not certain I agree with your numbers, but your thesis seems accurate."

"Well, maybe I was giving pastors more credit than they deserve for being able to deal very well with people. Perhaps I should have set the number at 30 or 40 instead of 50. You see, that's about the limit in the number of leaders or families a pastor can relate to very well. It is the pastor's job to expand his or her ministry by getting others involved in mission beyond the pastor's capabilities."

This conversation suggests interesting insights into pastoring vital churches. In the first place, the pastor's image of ministry must include equipping the saints for mission. The idea of controlling everything that goes on in a church, common to many pastors, is somehow eliminated in vital churches. Second, a pastor who feels that he or she can minister well to most people in a congregation needs to consider carefully human fallibility and emotion. This analysis of his or her capabilities will enable the pastor to be more realistic about the actual number of persons he or she may be able to reach effectively. Third, a pastor's attitude toward the church, toward Jesus Christ, and toward laypersons as ministers will greatly affect the possibility of a church's becoming a vital, witnessing community of believers.

The pastor of a vital congregation can increase its ministry or can make a thriving and vital congregation a dead ash. As the most visible of church leaders, the pastor controls the formal communication lines and interacts most often with elected and real leaders. These two control points, communication and the leadership core of a church, can make or break a church's program according to the direction it takes in regard to ministry and mission.

A more careful examination of several of the attributes of pastors who have been leaders of vital congregations will help clarify this point.

Positive and Optimistic

One of the most consistently striking characteristics of pastors of vital churches is their positive and optimistic outlook. They envision a strong future for their churches. They partly attribute this positivism to the desire of laypersons to learn more about the Bible and the church.

A core of laity interested in learning is the way one pastor described his congregation.

> They want to know how to live, and they study the Bible to find out. Not only that, once they find out what they should be doing, they try to do it. For example, this is not a very liberal community. But one of our Bible classes got excited about the passage in Matthew about feeding the hungry and clothing those without clothes. They helped start a campaign of concern that resulted in a mission in the midst of our worst crime area. Not only that, they helped organize a group that pressured the city government to fix up an old building near the corner for homeless people. Those aren't things a church of this stature is expected to do in this community. But our people got excited about the Bible and did what they felt was proper.

The pastor conveniently overlooked his behind-the-scenes support of these activities. While these endeavors were not his idea, he helped interpret their needs to other leaders and encouraged the church council to support the efforts of these laity. His positive encouragement and optimism that they could do something were very important in helping the programs become successful, according to the laity interviewed.

Less dramatic, but equally important, were reports that worship services were "alive." *Alive* is a hard word to codify in experience, but interviews indicate that it was the manner of the pastor that made the difference between an ordinary and a vital worship service. A positive pastor may preach the same sermon as one who is noncommittal, or even negative, but the results are quite different. The scripture passage used takes on meaning for the laity. The music becomes both soothing and challenging, and the sermon has truths that are hard to take, but easy to understand as part of God's requirements.

According to the laypersons interviewed, the congregations left the services with a feeling of God's presence. They confessed that they often came with troubles that seemed overwhelming, but after the service they felt that a way had been opened for them to handle whatever issue they confronted. They said that their help came not only from what the pastor said but also from the way the pastor's attitude spoke to them.

Their interpretation of being positive did not mean the pastor was soft or unrealistic. It meant that pastors with a positive outlook on life and an upbeat feeling about their churches convey a bounce to the life of parishioners. Death, illness, disease, and disappointment must still be faced, but they take on a different meaning when the pastor's attitude is positive about life. That positivism, according to both the pastor and the laity in these vital churches, came from their being in touch with God through Jesus Christ. That, by the way, is the first prerequisite for a minister of a vital church, mentioned earlier in this chapter.

The pastor who is positive is like that because of what he or she believes about God through the promises of Jesus Christ. Any pastor who is in continual contact with the Lord can be nothing but positive even in the face of the worst of life's challenges. It is this sense of the pastor's faith that people in vital churches point to as they speak of the pastor's positive attitude. No one who has touched the Master's hem can be anything but positive about the church, and its people's ministry is a reflection of being in touch with God.

Tone of Vitality

The people in vital congregations tried to separate the pastor's positive support of their work and the church's ministry from a sense of vitality. They felt that both were needed, but they also said the church was vital before a particular pastor came. While this separation might be evident to leaders in these churches, it is hard for an outsider to make the distinction. On the other hand, experience has shown that some pastors who have a positive attitude are not able to set a tone of vitality for their churches.

The first element in vitality is a sense of being part of something that is very important. Importance is measured in two ways, on a personal and on a group level. In vital churches, both ways are involved.

The individual is deemed important by the way he or she is greeted, is visited, is encouraged to attend church school and worship, and is involved in some sort of small group setting. In every way, the individual perceives that he or she is ministered to by the church and by other members. This is a prerequisite for ministry and is established by the pastor by example more than by dictate.

Groups are shown to be important by the manner in which they are used to express ministry within the congregation and mission in the community and the world. Small groups become vehicles for teaching, fellowship, and support within the congregation. These groups might be initiated as study or interest classes, but they are continued as a necessary addition to the program of the church. Once organized and given a life of their own, they are encouraged to participate in the mission of the church through volunteer activities or monetary support of particular outreach and mission projects in the community and in the world. While these two forms of vitality are encouraged, a third strand is running through the congregation. It is an emphasis on the vitality of the gathered, worshiping community. Although a vital congregation may have as many as four worship services or as few as one on any given Sunday, the theme of these services is the unified action of members as a witnessing body of believers. It is in the worship service(s) that the pastor's emphasis on vitality brings the individuals and the groups into a whole. They are encouraged *as a church* to engage in mission and in ministry, even though this may be done as individuals and as groups.

The sense of oneness of purpose within vital congregations comes about because the pastor sets a tone of vitality that unifies the congregation. This does not negate the separateness that comes because of loyalties to small groups or to attendance at a particular service. These loyalties are not tampered with by the pastor.

These pastors chose to discuss ministry and mission as being of the church and indicated that the specific activities expressing both mission and ministry would take several forms. Pastors incorporated members' natural tendencies toward parochialism into a feeling of being a part of something greater than a single group. Although they were small-group members, they also were members of a large group (the church) as they worked through their small group to express God's will in the world.

This emphasis on vitality of the whole set the tone for everything the church was about. It gave a meaning and a purpose to each activity. The tone was set by the pastor, and it was conveyed to others as the pastor was able to focus energies and attention on God's will for this church. This dimension of spirituality raised people from their normal selfish determinism to a higher plane of interest and concern for others. Without the pastor's emphasis on God's working through the church, however, the members would not have been lifted out of their narrowness into a more unified understanding of God's purpose for the church.

Strong Preaching

"How about preaching?"

"It is my single most important activity. I spend at least three days working on it, although the time spent in preparation is much longer. You see, my sermon topics are set several months in advance. In fact, I try to have my sermon ideas a year at a time."

"Isn't that constricting? What about emergency situations?"

"Look at it this way: Every Sunday morning is an emergency for some people. They come to church after a death in the family or a member of their family is ill or they are facing a job loss for themselves or someone in the family, and so forth. I believe, to be fair to them and to help them move through their pain and anxiety, that I owe them a carefully thought out interpretation of the scriptures. You can't do that in a few hours."

"I understand your thinking, but isn't it confining to (have your sermons planned for a year?"

"Perhaps I don't know what you mean by confining. Everything I do feeds into the sermons. My reading and studying obviously stimulate ideas and provide illustrations. Attendance at meetings and planning retreats stretch my mind and provoke new dimensions to the themes for sermons. My visiting in homes, offices, and hospitals gives me a feel for the people who will be at worship. How could any of these be confining? I feel that they are expanding my powers and opportunities as a communicator of the gospel."

This pastor of a 200 member congregation has the same kind of philosophy about preaching as did pastors in smaller and larger churches. All of them emphasized the need to be a strong preacher. None of them apologized for the amount of time and energy they spent in planning and preparing for their sermons. They all indicated that their interweaving of pastoral experiences into the sermons either by altering the direction of the sermon or through illustrations to bring home a particular point was important.

Laity spoke of strong preaching as a fact of their congregational life. Over the years, they had experienced strong, as well as mediocre and poor, preaching. They knew the difference in what they had now. It was strong, good preaching. In many cases, it may not have been as eloquent as some they have had, nor was it oratorical in the sense of being spellbinding. These people described it as strong. It contained the kinds of help and guidance they needed to get through their daily lives with a feeling of being true to the gospel. To a person, laity felt that the current pastor's strong preaching was a critical factor in the ability of this church to become and to remain vital.

As far as the research could ascertain, strong preaching consisted of solid biblical understanding enhanced by an interpretation useful to those who attended worship. Strong preaching depended on a liberal use of illustrations pertinent and understandable to the listeners. Laity were convinced that sermons must be based on scripture. Since many laypersons in these churches were attending Bible study, they were rather sophisticated in their understanding of Bible based sermons. The pastor could not shirk on preparation or study in this area. They also required relevancy for their own lives. They wanted interpretations they could take home with them, rather than phrases that might sound good but could not be used in daily experiences. They were practical about the preaching; it had to help them where they lived.

None of the vital church laypersons described their

117

pastors' preaching as the best oratory they had ever heard. They said that the sermon was delivered well and with conviction. These laypersons felt that they had the best kind of preacher—one who studied hard, who worked to make the scriptures come alive and be useful to their daily lives, and who spoke well. This combination, they knew from experience, is hard to find in most churches. It is probably hard to find because many pastors have not given preaching priority as their number one activity. In vital churches, preaching is the primary activity of the pastor because, as both pastors and laypersons said, that's what they were trained to do best, and that's where they have the most opportunity to spread the Word.

Mission Emphasis Essential

"One of the hardest tasks I have is to keep stretching these people beyond themselves. They do get involved in a lot of activities beyond the church, but it is easy to fall back into the rut of being self-centered."

"Why is it so important to be concerned with people who are not members of the church? Surely you have enough to do to minister effectively within the membership."

"The church was not established for its members. It was created to witness to the world. Jesus' admonition to the rich people, to the disciples, and to those who might want to follow was to look beyond themselves and their interests. They had to help others at all times."

"But if you took care of all the selfishness in the congregation and got them to look out for one another, you will have done what Jesus commanded."

"Not even close! Look at these people. Even by the most stringent of measures they are better off than most people in the world. Of course, every one of them will tell you they need more of this or that. But they tell you that as they sit in a home or apartment with furniture and heat. They may be out of money for a time, but there are avenues for them to get that, and people here will help them. But how about those who live in old rusted cars or on the streets? Who's helping them? Or families whose entire lives are spent moving from doorway to doorway and who eat from the garbage thrown away by others? Who's helping them? How about the children left to wander homeless through the years along the streets and junkyards of towns and cities? Isn't it a part of our responsibility to minister to them?"

"You have some good points, but I'm certain people in your membership will talk about dire needs among certain of your fellowship."

"You're correct. Our community has several pockets of need, and our congregation has a few. We aren't neglecting any of these. Yet, we are focusing our activities so that where we do our work, it will be effective. We want to make a difference. And we want the difference to be not only in our congregation but also along the streets of this town and in other places in this world."

This pastor has one of the major attributes of a leader in a vital congregation: She is interested in mission. In every congregation designated as vital, the mission emphasis was strong. It included activity in the community and in the world. Although much was happening that was focused on this church's ministry to members, a balance was struck with an emphasis beyond. Most of the time this emphasis required lay volunteers and asked for monetary support. In either case, the pastor was instrumental in helping people see beyond their local setting.

Interviewees in vital churches said that they needed the pastor's guidance to help them be actively concerned with others. It wasn't that they had no desire to assist. Rather, they felt that their intentions had to be channeled into constructive activities that required them to give time and money. Once these activities were in place, people were quite willing to become involved. It took the pastor†s assistance to help them focus and then to act before they could be in mission.

Another function of the pastor in vital congregations was to find appropriate types of mission activities for the church to support. This may sound like elitism, but it was not considered to be so. The pastor sought out mission opportunities that fit with the interests of the church. The pastor's suggestions were listened to because he or she was in touch with more kinds of mission enterprises than was any layperson.

The pastor, by promoting through sermons attendance at mission workshops for laypersons and by helping plan and produce mission fairs in the church, assisted laypersons to understand and to become interested in missions and community outreach. This function was done well. In fact, pastors in those congregations identified as vital in the studies liked this part of their roles very much.

Interpersonal Relations

A pastor of a vital congregation needs the normal skills of any good pastor. These skills include listening and hearing, managing conflict, leading in conflict resolution, administrative oversight, spiritual disciplines, public speaking, and getting along with people. Each pastor has these skills, although one or more of the skills may be more developed than the others.

The primary thing people in vital congregations mention about their pastor is her or his ability to demonstrate care and concern for them. This, according to laypersons, is shown by the fact that the pastor remembers their names and their family situations. There is a carryover of remembrance in conversations from one meeting to another, which gives the laypersons a feeling of being important to the pastor. These remembrances indicate to them that the pastor actually is concerned for them. It is difficult for many pastors to remember names or conversations over any period of time. The pastors of vital churches did not seem to have outstanding memories. They did interact with parishioners in a manner that was consistent and often. They made it their business to learn how to recall names of members as well as of visitors. They have discovered that names are important to everyone. It was especially important to remember names of visitors to a worship service.

The one impressive discovery about vital church pastors is that they were normal pastors with an abnormal interest in making their lives examples of Christ and their congregations places where people can grow in grace and practice the faith.

Calling and Teaching

Preaching, as has been noted, is a primary activity of pastors of vital churches. They bolster their teaching by calling on their members. Each pastor in the vital churches studied had a schedule for home and hospital visitation. This was true in urban, suburban, exurban, rural, and county seat communities. Pastors of vital churches called during the day and at least three evenings a week.

Pastors in vital congregations do not do all of the home visitation conducted in the churches. Laypersons have much responsibility for visitation, especially to contact visitors and to identify potential new members. Pastors, however, do not retreat to their studies and busy themselves with counseling. They believe it is necessary for them to be among their people, especially during illnesses and stressful times in their lives. Hospital visitation is an extremely important time for visiting for these pastors.

Visitation pushes the pastors into certain kinds of teaching. Most of them during the year will teach one Bible study class. This may be conducted during Lent or the fall and will be open to the entire congregation. It may be part of an extensive adult education program, or it may be most of the adult education program for the church. The size of the church determines how extensive the adult education program will be and how often the pastor may teach during a year.

Pastors will often teach a second course during the year. This will be a shortened course and may range from church history to a social problem. The idea for the course often comes as a result of the visiting the pastor does among the parishioners. The two activities, calling and teaching, are symbiotic. They nourish each other.

Church Is Focus of Ministry

Every one of the pastors in vital churches was ambitious. They were aware of their status within the denomination and within their region. On the other hand, few of them voiced any concern about the attitudes of other ministers toward them or the attitude of those who might be in positions of power in the national or regional parts of their denomination. Pastors of vital congregations, on the other hand, were very much concerned that their churches would personify Christ.

It was surprising to discover this emphasis within this set of clergy. Their congregations had become known as alive and forward looking. Colleagues were somewhat envious of the number of programs and people involved in them.

Yet these colleagues pointed to extenuating circumstances that made the congregations vital. The pastors of the vital churches knew the congregation was alive because they, the pastors, poured themselves into its life. None of the pastors in vital churches said that they were unwilling to move. At the same time, none of them wanted to leave their church. They were happy and convinced that the Lord had called them to minister there at this time.

In the sense that they were satisfied, they were committed to making certain that the gospel message took form in their church. Their ministry was for this church at the present and the near future. None of them was content with the program because each had a dream for new programs. Yet, they were unwilling to suggest that the churches had reached their zenith and that it may be time for them to find other places for ministry.

The normal politics of power within the denomination seemed absent from, or at least subdued among, these pastors. They did not appear to want or to need to be involved. They wanted to do their job in this church.

The single-mindedness of these pastors was a common backdrop for their ministry and their church. It is doubtful that a congregation can become vital and remain alive if the pastor's interest strays from the focus on ministry in the church he or she is serving.

VIII

Leading Questions

It takes hard and continuous work to have and maintain a vital congregation. Lay leaders and the pastor in congregations need to review regularly the goals and accomplishments of their church's program and to project new areas of ministry among the many opportunities available to them. People call such processes by various names, including planning, prioritizing, envisioning, and futuring. Whatever the name given to your process is, it is essential to engage in it at least annually.

An analysis of a church's program must not become wrapped up in internal diagnosis. The purposes of such an analysis are to identify opportunities for mission and ministry, to determine how well the church is doing ministry in the areas it has chosen, and to decide which of the existing and new opportunities it should work at during the next two to five years.

Workbooks for planning the future are available from most denominations. These can be used to guide a church in a particular process. The following questions can be used also in thinking through in study groups, in planning retreats, or in a leadership council the directions a congregation desires to move in ministry and mission.

1. What do we want this church to be and to be doing in ministry and mission five years from now? What is our mission? What are the components of our ministry? How do all of these fit into a plan for mission and ministry for our congregation?
2. What must be changed in order to accomplish the ministry and mission we want to be engaged in five years from now?
3. What are the three most important activities of our church now that must be retained and improved in order to be part of its ministry and mission five years from now?
4. What kinds of leaders do we need? Where will we find them? How will they be trained? Who will train them?
5. What can be done in worship to make it more alive and spiritual? Who will make those changes?
6. Are there possibilities and/or need for changes in the music program? Do we have enough choirs? How will changes be implemented?
7. Do members understand and practice discipleship? How can they be strengthened in their concepts and practices of discipleship? Where can stewardship of time and money be undergirded and enhanced?
8. What might we do to enlarge our adult Christian education program so that it becomes a strong learning base for members? So that it is varied enough to allow people to enter into the life of the congregation? So that its classes might be a network of caring cells within the membership?
9. What can each member do to make and to keep

this church vital and growing in the Spirit of Christ? What can the church do to ensure each member's spiritual growth?

10. How can we strengthen the mission and outreach activities of the congregation? What kinds of opportunities for volunteer service should be opened for the members? Does this church need to start an outreach program for people in the neighborhood and/or community? How can we cooperate with other congregations in this kind of activity?

11. How can the lay leaders and the pastor work together to accomplish our goals in ministry and mission? Do we need a change of pastors? Do we need a tenure system for our leaders? Do we need better and more frequent opportunities for the exchange of ideas and hopes between our pastor and our leaders?

These are leading questions that congregations can find stimulating and exciting during discussions. The answers of the pastor, leaders, and members of a congregation can lead to renewal of purpose and increased commitment within the Body of Christ to doing ministry in the name of Jesus Christ. Even though these questions are used to look closely at the program, ministry, and mission of a congregation, until it discovers that its purpose is to spread the gospel of God's grace and love through Christ in this community and throughout the world, its vitality will be little more than a clanging cymbal.